# The Grand House
# at
# Swan Hill

## Fahey Harris

The Ninderry Press

2002

ISBN 0-95 80799-4-3

Book Title:
The Grand House at Swan Hill

Author:
Fahey Harris

Cover artist:
Mark Ambroz

Editor:
Dr Austin's Literary Clinic

First published in Brisbane, Australia by The Ninderry Press in August, 2002

A man travels the world over
in search of what he needs
and returns home to find it.

**George Moore** (1852–1933)

# Chapter One

I know precious little of my father's father. He died around the time I was born. That was so many eons ago now, those wrinkled enough to answer questions about him are as thin on grey matter as they are on the ground. He was born at Woolwich in Kent, England, around 1884-5. From that point on, I have no idea how he came to be a fireman in Brisbane in 1914.

The little I fathomed from my aging mother's memory about her father-in-law reveals a community-spirited man and a regular blood-donor to boot. He was active in Brisbane's public arenas, particularly the Buffalo Club and the Labor Party. The Labour Movement worldwide was barely out of negotiating the abolition of slavery in those days. Its Australian birthplace was a shearers' strike in Barcaldine, Queensland, in the late 1800s.

Grandfather Fred's passion, it seems, was sailing. He was President of the Brisbane Restricted Sailing Club. Whilst his love of water flowed down to my father, it definitely dried up before reaching me. Apparently, he was extraordinarily well read. After his death, Archbishop Duhig purchased his extensive personal library. Mum remembers him as a rather dapper Englishman who charmed the ladies, including her and her sister. His impeccable manners and style held them in thrall, as he escorted them to tea at Webster's Inn.

Webster's was typical of a number of teashops in Brisbane during that era. Only the Shingle Inn remains - a memento of a time when no self-respecting woman would be seen in public without her hat and gloves.

Fred's wife, Mary lived into my early twenties. So I relish some sublime first-hand memories concerning my paternal grandmother. I knew her as 'Nanny' and recall a diminutive, generous, snowy-haired lady who spent most of her time around her Fortitude Valley haunts. She cherished the Valley ambience. Rummaging for bargains in secondhand shops was a great passion. I confess it's a trait both my sister and I appear to have inherited.

Far from hoarding her bargains, once she had *bagged her game* she was only too happy to give it away. In fact, she delighted in bestowing some newfound treasure upon the vaguest of acquaintances.

Mum paints the detail of a time Nanny offered her a gorgeous, burgundy *chaise longue*. She had snapped it up for a pittance on a secondhand store jaunt. Mother felt reluctant to deprive her of such an impressive piece, so she declined with thanks. On her next visit to the mother-in-law, she noted the long lounge's absence. Nanny had donated it to some passing acquaintance lucky enough to have admired it.

Nanny was a devout Catholic, regularly attending Mass at the Crypt. That site has now been redeveloped as Cathedral Place apartments and shops. She was the sole daughter of Irish settlers, drawn by the gold seams of Charters Towers in 1889. In the nineteenth century, Charters was Queensland's second-largest town. Its streets while rumoured to be paved with gold were, in fact, lined with *art nouveau riche* Victorian buildings. The nearby goldfields were the most productive in the state and they provided a mighty affluence. The stock exchange in Charters, I read, had no less than three calls a day!

It would be interesting to know how Mary ended up in Brisbane, married to some fellow from Kent. Perhaps some questions are better left unasked.

At my father's birth in 1914, Mary and Frederick living in High Street, Lutwyche moved to Stratton Street in Newstead. Long-term residents of Brisbane may remember the huge gasometers. They loomed large on the skyline of Newstead for most of the twentieth century. While a mere tot, I distinctly recall overhearing the comment: *anyone living within sniffing distance of the gasometers would be likely to end up a sandwich short of a picnic.* (This had me suspiciously sniffing my sandwiches for some time.) Looking back, I believe there may have been some substance to the theory.

Fred and Mary remained in Stratton Street until Fred died, toward the end of the forties. At the time of his death he was employed by the Workers' Education Association Library. He left Nanny impoverished with two adult sons. My father was more than a decade older than his brother.

When I recall Nanny now, the images centre on times mum and I used to visit her. I can still see her topping up the remaining milk with an inch of water so there would be enough to go around for the cuppa. I was quite impressed by how tricky this was. From my child's perspective, it still looked like milk - yet twice as much! She was, by then, living as a widow in a sea of identically small, grey fibro-cottages near what is now Victoria Park.

These dwellings were built as airforce barracks during the war. They were subsequently used for housing the less fortunate. Nanny evidently fell into that category.

My memories include a mysterious duck pond.

One of my most incongruous flashbacks comes from her absolute insistence that her husband's brother was a grandfather to one of The Beatles. He shared a surname. I was in my early teens when The Beatles rose to fame, so I clung desperately to the hope of it being true. I regularly impressed my peers at Kelvin Grove High School with this tenuous connection. Apparently, Nanny even went as far as to write to the last known address of her husband's brother in England. (I doubt she received a reply.)

Towards the end of her life, Nanny was forced to move from her convenient lodgings near Victoria Park Golf Course to alternative government housing at Sticksville (Zillmere, to be precise). This must have coincided with the barracks' demolition to create open parkland. It's curious how the whole precinct has now become millionaire mansions, squashed into a chic-to-chic residential zone. There's still an expansive green belt encompassing sports fields and the duck pond - although that looks more like a puddle now and not a bit mysterious.

Moving way out of town put Nanny so far from her favourite haunts in the Valley, she became sadly out of sorts. The relocation was made all the more distressing by her younger son's recent admission to the mental institution at Goodna. To someone living in Zillmere in those days, Goodna was dangerously close to the edge of the world. The clinical term for my uncle's condition is paranoid schizophrenia.

I have a distant memory of visiting him at Goodna. Glimpses of moments, revived whenever I see a television news-report about the direful state of public-health facilities in Queensland. With their cutting-edge indifference they open a weeping sore by showing his buildings and grounds. Externally, the place seems to have changed little in the intervening forty plus years.

From Zillmere, Nanny managed to find her way back to a humble low-set timber bungalow in Union Street, in her beloved Spring Hill. There she remained until the late sixties, when failing health necessitated a move to the Eventide retirement home at Sandgate.

The last I saw of her was at the then Chermside Chest Hospital. I was with my mother. I doubt Nanny was aware of us. Her tiny body was almost lost in the hospital bed as she writhed in grotesque pain.

Within the next few days, mum and I were back to collect the small tin box of her meagre possessions. It represented her life of over eighty years. Most of it was old photographs and letters (none from England to connect me with fame and fortune, alas). She was buried at Toowong cemetery next to her husband, Frederick, in February '72.

Her younger son may have been institutionalised at the time, at any rate I don't recall seeing him at his mother's funeral.

My memories of that uncle are obscure. Mum's recollections are also hazy. She tells me my father and his younger brother were anything but close. She remembers her brother-in-law as a peculiar and 'rather shifty' character. He quickly squandered a small inheritance from his father although, in his defence, this was far from extraordinary behaviour for a fellow in his early twenties. He was, however, particularly remiss in his attitude towards his struggling, widowed mother. He deliberately avoided her as she waited for him to donate a little of his pension each fortnight.

He was prone to wandering about the Valley and Newstead precincts sporting a hat with an assortment of flags in the band. He would wear on his person, like trophies of war, his father's medals for services to the Buffalo Club. Back then, togged up in such attire he would have attracted a deal of attention. (These days in the Valley he wouldn't rate a second glance.)

He never married. Although he had spent at least two stints as a psych patient, he clearly wasn't restricted to this rôle.

I caught sight of him around the place, some years after the original Goodna visit as a child. The first occasion, I was in my mid-teens working in an office at Newstead close to Stratton Street. I recognised my father's brother crossing the street just ahead. I collapsed with relief he hadn't noticed me. At that age I was much too self-conscious to lay claim to a relative whose appearance and behaviour was so bizarre.

I think I glimpsed him once more in my late twenties. He was on the other side of Edward Street in amongst the hurly-burly of the city. I didn't exactly rush into the traffic to identify him. If indeed that was my uncle then, by this stage, he had all the trappings of vagrancy including the *bottle in a brown paper bag* item. I never laid eyes on him again. I suppose he would be well and truly inspirited by now. That's the pathetic sum of my knowledge concerning dad's side of the family.

8

# Chapter Two

My mother's father was a stubborn and belligerent Irishman called by his friends, Paddy Fitzgerald. To me he was always just, Pa. Actually, he wasn't born in Ireland despite displaying all the unrivalled singularities of Paddy expatriates. At the end of the 1800s, his parents moved from County Cork to Monklands, near the Gympie goldfields. Gympie was a boomtown, as towns boomed in those days, being the premier gold-rush magnet in Queensland. As the gold ran out so did many of its residents. They searched all the way to Brisbane and further afield for work.

Many rose to prominence in the community, including one Andrew Fisher, Prime Minister of Australia on no less than three occasions between 1907 and 1915.

Pa was born in 1887, arriving in a teeming family toward the end of a decade of children, with a tally of seven females. They were a colourful bunch from all accounts. One of his brothers, Jack died at the age of twelve in a horse-and-cart accident. His death left Paddy just one remaining adult brother, Fergus. The family moved from Monklands to Brookes Street, Fortitude Valley in the early 1900s. On arriving in Brisbane, Paddy found a job as a shunter on the railways.

Paddy used to be a keen sportsman in those days. There was a boxing trophy won while a youngster in Monklands. However, his real achievements were on the football field. He represented both his state and country in Rugby Union before changing to Rugby League. An old scrapbook I found lying around the house documents his career.

The "Natives" won the local Club Premiership with Paddy on side. When Queensland went to Sydney, he played forward against a NSW team that included the legendary 'Dally' Messenger. His team was beaten sixty-five to nine. Positions were radically changed for the second game. But Paddy kept his spot! They lost again, thirty-two to four.

When the Queensland team returned to the Brisbane Cricket Ground that year, they played a visiting Kiwi side. In spite of losing both games to the Kiwis, Paddy played well enough to make the Australian team. He played alongside the great 'Dally' Messenger and Australia won the match 13-10!

He played for Queensland against New Zealand in the first game of the series. On this occasion he was halfback. Queensland lost. He was in the pack for the next Queensland versus New Zealand encounter, which turned out to be his last representative game of Rugby League.

Apparently, he formed a rapport with visiting Kiwis who taught him the fearsomely impressive *Haka*. I know this for a fact because he passed the extraordinary ritual to my young brother, who sometimes renders a stirring performance as a party trick.

Rumour had it he was selected to tour Britain but refused. One theory for his rebuttal was that he couldn't afford months off work. As far as I'm concerned, the more credible version was his reluctance to make the long sea voyage. An aversion to water was the only trait Paddy and I shared.

Before continuing with Pa's story, it's polite and appropriate to introduce you to the woman he was eventually to marry.

# Chapter Three

Both my mother and her sister saw me as the spitting image of their mother, Rebecca. I suppose if I look close enough at her photo on the wall, I can see some resemblance. The old, framed portrait was shot in England in the late 1800s when Rebecca was a teenager. I never had the pleasure of her acquaintance; she passed on years before I pushed through. From Cromer, in Norfolk she derived from Jewish parentage. In her late teens she left her family, of one remaining brother.

Dallying for awhile in France, she was eventually to describe the Parisians as a trifle too arrogant for her liking.

It was to alleviate the pain of a condition exacerbated by cold that she then opted for warmer climes.

The strata of English society with which she identified typically drops the H. Most of my life, I had pronounced Maiden Hair Fern as Maiden Air Fern, that being the way it was interpreted by my mother from hers. It was only when I saw the plant named in a nursery that I caught on. (I still prefer Maiden Air's quietly ethereal quality.)

Rebecca's search for salutary warmth eventually brought her to Queensland. She met and married a fellow from Gympie, who worked as a shunter on the railways alongside a man named Paddy. That same Paddy would one day become my grandfather.

Not long after Rebecca's first marriage, she set off for South Africa, fresh spouse in hand (who had vowed to make her a fortune in the mines). For awhile this move afforded them a lifestyle bountiful enough to include live-in servants. Their son, Benjamin was born a Springbok.

When her husband exhibited the initial symptoms of Miner's Complaint (pneumoconiosis) they returned to Brisbane.

They set up in the Valley, selling ostrich feathers for ladies' hats.

Unfortunately, his condition deteriorated as rapidly as the fashion for ostentatious headgear, and the feathers were forced to go cheap. The sale was finalised in a pre-emptive financial deal by a large department store called Overell's.

When Rebecca's husband died, she was left a penniless widow with a ravenous child. She found a live-in housekeeping position at the

Presbytery of St. Joseph's College at Gregory Terrace. This gave her a modest income and a roof over the head of her stripling consumer.

She was living at the Presbytery when Paddy first courted her. Paddy lost his milk-teeth around Gympie, as had Rebecca's late husband; the two worked on the railways together. Yet, only a barefaced liar could describe them as friends. Paddy would never have numbered a member of the Masonic Lodge among his chums (as was Rebecca's late husband). He abhorred what he considered 'that club of belligerent Protestant bastards'.

His visits to the widow culminated in discussions of marriage. Before that step could be taken, however, Rebecca would have to convert to Catholicism. She did this with a great flourish of conviction. Soon after, Paddy married her in St. Stephen's Church in Brisbane and adopted her son. The family moved into a rented cottage in Kennigo Street, Spring Hill.

The place was still there, last time I drove past.

# Chapter Four

Rebecca was already thirty-five and four years her husband's senior when she gave birth to Paddy's first child, in 1918. They called that little girl Ella, after Paddy's mother. She was to be my mother. Towards the end of Ella's first year, the family moved to another rented house. It was further out of town, north along Gympie Road not far from the tram terminus at Bowen Bridge. The bridge was a simple wooden structure in those days. The area beyond, known as Swan Hill was still quite undeveloped.

A smattering of dwellings and shops were girded by paddocks. If you can believe the stories from old-timers Breakfast Creek, in those days, carried clean water and supported an abundance of fish. I have it on good authority: a net could be dragged across the creek to fish more than you could possibly eat. (Caution was needed to avoid catfish.)

There were numerous swimming-holes with pebbled bottoms and pristine white, sandy banks. Here the neighbourhood kids entertained themselves diving, swimming and playing Two Up.

At the time of their relocation to Swan Hill, Paddy was working as a carter for Dalgety's. Of course, a carter needed horses to ply his trade. So Paddy was bound to purchase a couple of Clydesdales. The horses were agisted in the paddock at the back of the grocery store, directly opposite their rental. These lodgings were quite adequate for their current needs. Upstairs, there were three modestly proportioned bedrooms, a small, unpretentious dining area, a relatively spacious kitchen (compared with the rest of the house) and an open-front verandah. Downstairs, an all-purpose washroom was hidden in the corner of a forest of tall, wooden stumps. A thunder-box kept regular traffic up the backyard. It was the classic high-set worker's cottage of the era.

The only blot on the domestic-bliss landscape was the bloke next door. Wouldn't you know - he turned out to be a member of the Masonic Lodge! Naturally, Paddy and he took an instant aversion. They regularly hurled abuse and the occasional object. If Paddy happened to be feeling particularly windy after a few beers, he would yell through the side window into his neighbour's house:

'Masons walk knee deep in Catholic blood!'

In between the feuding both families managed to cobble together their respective lives. Within three years, Paddy and Rebecca had another daughter, Cecelia. Their tenure in the modest rented house was drawing to a close when Paddy's first son was born.

They named the boy Jack (in memory of Paddy's kid brother who died tragically at twelve). By the time Jack came on the scene, Paddy and Rebecca had saved 75 pounds. It was just the amount needed to buy the two 16-perch blocks opposite, where he had agisted his horses. Shortly after, a rough carpenter, or 'an R.C.,' in Paddy's dialect, started on The Grand House design. A sizeable mortgage and several months later, Paddy and his family made the short move across the street, out of their humble worker's cottage and into the grandeur of their new residence. The year was 1925.

The Grand House at Swan Hill perched imperiously on lofty wooden stumps. Straddling two blocks, it resembled an exotic clipper in a sea of worker-cottage barges. A sturdy weatherboard structure of generous proportions, its exteriors were regimented by mission brown. A blazing silver-frosted tin roof skylit the dark mocha colour.

Here's Rebecca to guide you round the house, now.

*A stroll up the impressive front stairs, featuring a deck midway - if you'll just follow me - leads to these ornate lattice-doors of the front verandah. Before we proceed, cast an eye towards the timber balustrades. Note, if you will, the feature motif - a timber insert of an art deco tulip, très chic. A bit of flair is always a real welcome, whereas a welcome mat is just a cliché, wouldn't you say?*

*Bang in the middle of the impressive entry door is this beautiful brass doorknocker in the shape of a lion's 'ead. It takes no end of spit and polish to keep it gleaming! The large, scarlet centre-pane contrasts strikingly with the petite, side inserts of sapphire blue. The glass rainbows light brilliantly, like shattered diamonds when touched by the afternoon sun.*

*After you, please, as we step inside. The dark, ever so long 'allway is framed at the end by an ornate wooden archway. Each of the three panelled doors opening off this spacious 'all is crowned with artistically fret-worked timber air-vents, echoing the deco tulip design. C'est très joli, n'est ce pas?*

*This first door takes us to this generously proportioned sleeping quarter, though not the biggest within as you'll soon discover. Its glamorous windowpane overlooks the front garden. 'Ere, let me draw*

14

*the curtains fully for you. The frangipani makes a spectacular display at this time of the year. Did you notice 'ow the colours of the glass in the front door are replicated in the side panels of this picturesque casement? These sash-windows are so easy to slide up, as the old grandfather-clock weights descend inside their shafts like dumb-waiters.*

*I bumped into a few of them on the ship over 'ere, an' all*

*This second door on the right down the 'all conceals another bedroom, slightly smaller than the former. Its window 'as a lovely outlook to the side garden, where the sweet peas will be in full bloom again in no time. The remaining door in the 'allway, over 'ere on the left, opens to reveal the piéce de rèsistance among bedrooms. Our boudoir, as you see is an enormous room with two sets of French doors opening onto sweeping front and side verandahs. These doors feature symmetrical glass inserts with scarlet and sapphire colours replicating the front door's design. Paddy will be back presently so perhaps we'd better 'ead off once more into the 'allway.*

*Beyond this ornate wooden archway is the dining room. A picture rail circumscribes the wall about a foot below the expansive VJ ceilings, segmenting the lofty walls. Nice touch, I think. These 'ighly polished redgum floors throughout set this huge Indian rug off in the dining room right regally. A smaller, fourth bedroom, though certainly adequate can be accessed just 'ere at the end of the dining room. Any deficiencies in this room's size are fully compensated by its direct access to the side verandah.*

*Those wooden blinds over the verandah openings are designed to be rolled up and secured to let in breeze and light. On sultry nights, they allow enough privacy for a mattress to be thrown onto the side verandah affording balmier more star-struck sleeping - a favourite indulgence I must admit.*

*A roomy kitchen adjoining the dining room completes the upper deck. This functional area comes equipped with a modern wood-stove in its chimney recess. Even more contemporary is this lovely ice-chest. Called a Mawson, this marvellous invention refrigerates after a block of ice is placed in the top, accessed by lifting this lid. From the top, a pipe runs down the back of the wooden cabinet to a collecting tray on the floor. The tray is neatly concealed by a lift up board. Perishable items stored in this wooden cabinet remain kosher as long as the ice is replaced regularly. We enjoy the convenience of daily ice deliveries around this way.*

*The latest in over'ead gas-fittings illuminates the kitchen and dining room as required. To light these, one needs only to balance carefully on a chair in order to gain the necessary altitude for the 'igh ceiling jets. 'Aving completed our spin around the upper deck let's proceed down below.*

*These rear stairs run from the dining room to the under 'ouse. It's a bit low so 'duck or grouse,' as they say. Paddy 'as been known to 'ang the meat safe rather carelessly at times, much to the detriment of 'is poor cranium. 'E don't 'alf make a racket when it 'appens! After I've been cooking up a storm in the kitchen I store me chutneys in the meat safe to cool. You'll observe that the under 'ouse flooring, as you would expect, is dirt.*

*Just beyond the triple-basin concrete wash-tubs, there's a concrete slab wash'ouse over 'ere in the back corner. Being encased on the outside with tin and on the inside with fibro, it's both cosy and private. Perfect for the weekly ablutions.*

*Isn't the huge iron bath perched regally on eagle-claws clasping them golden-globes simply spectacular? Cleopatra Woz Ere is artfully graffitied on the side. Paddy assures us this is absolutely authentic! Just outside the bathroom in the open backyard is a wood-fired copper boiler. Conveniently positioned to facilitate 'auling buckets of 'ot water both to the bathroom and the concrete washing tubs.*

*The W.C., which is emptied by night gangs, is a discreet distance up the backyard.*

*The stables are solid and sizeable enough to comfortably accommodate both the Clydesdales. Naturally, there's the chook 'ouse, also a substantial structure. When those mandarin, mulberry and mango trees reach their full potential, there'll be no shortage of fruit for the sideboard, either.*

*I'll let you out quietly down the side lane before Paddy comes 'ome. Mind the thorns on those rose bushes as you brush past. They're Queen Victoria variety, don't you know! My! Doesn't that jasmine vine over the front gate smell delightful? Don't forget to shut the gate.*

The day Rebecca moved in, she proudly hung the picture of her youthful self (taken in England many years earlier) on the dining-room wall. She must have felt she was the envy of the rapidly expanding neighbourhood. The tramline had already been extended further along Gympie Road, past the Windsor Council Chambers.

A proliferation of grocery and butcher shops sprung up to service a growing community. Butchers typically spread sawdust over their floors. The entry was fitted with a light, mesh swing-door to keep the 'butchers' canaries' (blowflies) out.

My mother was almost seven when the family moved into The Grand House. At that stage, the household consisted of Paddy and Rebecca, their three children, as well as Paddy's adopted son and the houseguest.

To elaborate on the houseguest, I'll need to digress to a few years earlier. This is back when Paddy and Rebecca were still living at Kennigo Street, Spring Hill with their first-born daughter and her half-brother. Another childhood friend of Paddy's called on them after fleeing Gympie. His *refugee* status was Category A: he had just been jilted at the altar. Paddy and Rebecca invited him to stay while he got over the shock. He became Ella's godfather and remained with the family for the rest of his life. My mother always speaks with great affection about the houseguest who worked as a wharfie. He must have been grateful for a home, and expressed it by being exceptionally helpful and kind to Rebecca and her children.

He planted and maintained a large vegetable patch in the backyard. He was also responsible for the mulberry, mandarin and mango trees around the back and side yards. The row of glorious Queen Victoria rose bushes at the front was his doing. It was he who purchased Ella's first port, when she started at the nearby Catholic school.

He may also have been responsible for Ella's lifelong love of a flutter on the horses. It seems our houseguest was a bit regular at the nearby Kedron Park races. He would put a halfpenny on something Ella liked the look of. As you might imagine, on that basis it didn't take long for Ella to develop more than a cursory interest in the punt.

Although, it could well have been some rogue shamrock-shaped gene: Paddy also loved to gamble on equestrian odds.

# Chapter Five

Extreme financial hardship was ever imminent in the boom-and-bust decades of the early twentieth century. Those out of work were obliged to take the camel and pack lunches to reach Petrie for five-shilling relief money. With a shortage of camels, most resorted to Shanks's pony. That surely took an inordinate amount of time and shoe leather from Swan Hill. Nevertheless, it must have been worthwhile considering the number, including the houseguest and assorted neighbours, who undertook the voyage during the Great Depression.

Work was intermittent for both Paddy and the houseguest. Rebecca used to sell eggs and chooks around the neighbourhood. Ella recalls her mother being frighteningly adept with an axe (at least when required to decapitate a chook, before swiftly and skilfully removing the feathers for a sale). This was quite some departure from her lifestyle in South Africa not so many years earlier.

Paddy had a number of influential friends in Brisbane. They were in the main, old school chums from Gympie drawn to the big smoke where they had prospered. One was a judge who received the tribute of a city street being named after him. The two regularly drank at a pub in town, often with another school chum from Gympie. He had climbed the corporate ladder to an executive position with Dalgety's.

Paddy no longer knew the security of full-time employment, so he jumped at every chance of subcontract carting for Dalgety's. On these occasions, his old friend would seize the opportunity to implore Paddy to join the Masonic Club and enhance his prospects. Paddy ruggedly stymied the logic of anyone even attempting to talk sensibly about such a thing.

Locals bonded into close-knit communities during those teeth-clenching times of the Great Depression. Rebecca became a prime mover in one instance. She had a friend, a Mrs. O'Shea who lived just up the street. When Rebecca learned that her friend's family faced eviction from their rental, she resolved to assist. Her chance came after hearing on the grapevine that the worker's cottage, on a 16-perch block adjoining The Grand House was soon to be vacated.

Rebecca begged, borrowed and scrounged funds for one week's rent. With this, she pushed a foot in the door for her friend's family.

This family, incidentally, consisted of Rebecca's girlfriend, her husband, their daughter (who was a little older than Ella) and a gaggle of younger boys.

Mind you, it wasn't uncommon for Rebecca to be on the receiving end of community generosity. One of the local shopkeepers regularly extended her hamper: her weekly grocery delivery unfailingly included a free bag of broken biscuits or lollies.

That particular shopkeeper was also a local-government councillor. To this day there's a park bearing his name not far from The Grand House. He fathered an enormous family, all domiciled at the back of his grocery store from where they supplied a live-in workforce.

He had so many sons they formed their own cricket team. Their team would regularly challenge a combined side of locals. The benevolent shopkeeper's brother owned a house in the next street, their blocks sharing a boundary at the back. That brother also spawned several sons and daughters; so the family generated a veritable tribe in the district of Swan Hill.

Paddy being one of many siblings, it followed Ella had a few cousins strewn around. An Aunt Maggie who moved to Paddington, Sydney, warrants special mention. Her son was nicknamed 'Red Ted,' alluding to his politics. The Communist Party was alive and well in the days of the Depression. Red Ted was a wharfie.

Paddy had no fewer than four old-maid sisters working as schoolteachers in the area. It's curious how the academic attributes of the female Fitzgeralds contrast so starkly the less than scholarly characteristics of the surviving sons.

Fergus at least had a degree of *streetwise*. As for Paddy, he possibly suffered one too many blows to the brain during his formative years in Gympie as a competitive boxer.

Fergus's nickname was 'Fiftybob.' For awhile, he occupied a house that shared part of its back boundary with The Grand House. *Fiftybob* Fergus had two boys. The elder was Martin, the younger, Jack. Jack, like Paddy's son, was named in memory of his late Uncle Jack who died, while only a boy, in Gympie.

Ella viewed Fiftybob with some suspicion after the night she came home with her family to find all his furniture under their house. Quite coincidentally, that same night, Fiftybob's house burnt to the ground. 'Rats' were cited on the insurance claim as the likely cause.

# Chapter Six

It can have been no bed of roses being married to a man like Paddy, whose preferred pastimes were drinking and fighting in that order. He kept a slate at the Queen's Hotel, near Dalgety's offices in the city, where he collected his pay on Fridays. Good times or bad that slate would be wiped clean before Rebecca (waiting patiently outside) was given any housekeeping. His other watering hole was the Exhibition Hotel at Spring Hill. This was a popular place for veteran footballers to congregate and roar over past triumphs. The publican was a fellow called Tommy Gorman - the *Wally Lewis* of his era.

After Paddy had a skinful, along with a probable punch up, Tommy Gorman would bundle him off home. Sometimes he would be alone on this staggering journey. At others, he may have had the company of his best friend and Irish drinking buddy, Mickey O'Rourke.

Mickey also had wife and kids waiting at home, up the road from The Grand House. At times, Mickey's wife became so enraged by her husband's drinking, she resorted to having his name put on the pub's blackboard. In those days, such an action meant the publican could be heavily fined for serving those listed.

Rebecca regularly fulminated on the need to do likewise with her husband. They proved to be hollow threats.

In the earliest days, when Paddy's mode of transport was his horse-drawn delivery wagon, Tommy Gorman would bundle him and Mickey into the cart before placing the reins into Paddy's hands. With a hearty slap on the old Clydesdale's rump, coupled with the appropriate *eeeeyup* bellowed at shatteringly beery decibels, the horse would ably haul its stewed cargo back along the byways home.

A few years down the track, after Paddy had traded in the Clydesdale and cart for a Model-T Ford, Ella was bewildered as to how it too, managed the task. Paddy could be clearly heard along the dirt-street, informing several neighbourhoods at a time of his impending arrival with an erratic rendition of some nonsensical Irish ditty. One such enchanting piece of verse went something like:

*Once upon a time*
*when the birds shit lime*

*and the monkeys*
*chewed tobacco;*
*the little boy run*
*with his finger up his bum*
*to see what was*
*the matta.*

On hearing this raucous gibberish, Rebecca would swiftly command the kids to move off the street. In this inebriated state, Paddy would often denigrate Rebecca as *the English Jew* and rebuke her for spoiling her eldest son, Benjamin.

Paddy's T-Model was invaluable during elections. Being a staunch Labor man, Paddy willingly offered his truck for campaigning. In the evenings the T-Model, alight with hurricane lamps, could be descried on various street corners. Politician comrades would be spruiking hollow promises from their temporary platform on the tray-back whilst Paddy, in all likelihood, would be throwing punches at anyone in the crowd drunk enough to argue back.

To give him his due, Paddy was always respectably dressed for a drink (or a fight). He never set foot out the house without first highly polishing his boots, putting on his dark suit and starched white shirt. He invariably wore the same crochet black tie, finishing the outfit with an Akubra. Mind you, by the time he made it home after a Saturday evening at the pub, his appearance was distinctly less polished. Rebecca would brush and straighten out his hat, before placing it neatly back on top of the cupboard in readiness for next Saturday's outing.

There's a story about a time Paddy fell from the car at the bottom of the back steps and knocked himself out. Rebecca fetched the ambulance, which took him to the general hospital. On the way there he rallied and, still intoxicated, struck up with his usual carry on - singing, giving recitals and gratuitous advice on where to stick things. With this he was promptly placed into Ward 16, at which point he dozed off once more. (For those unfamiliar with Brisbane, Ward 16 was for the severely reality challenged.)

When he woke up the next morning as to his whereabouts, he jumped out of bed and bolted down the road on foot to The Grand House. In his haste, he overlooked the fact that he was still wearing his hospital-issue pyjamas.

Incidentally, Paddy's T-Model was one of the earliest in the district. It came from the U.S. in a couple of big wooden crates. The instructions directed the purchaser to assemble the floor-seat and sides of the back tray using the packing cases. Many years later, when the vehicle was well past its use-by date, because he couldn't bring himself to part with it Paddy dug a hole and buried it up the backyard.

# Chapter Seven

Within three years of moving into The Grand House, Rebecca was expecting, again. She was distressingly ill this time and spent almost six months bedridden, living solely on a diet of gruel and barley water. More often than not the houseguest, who remained a pillar of strength to the family, would prepare this punitive diet.

In October 1927, her last child was born. He was a ginger-haired boy they called Fergus after Paddy's brother, Fiftybob. By now Rebecca and Paddy had two daughters and two sons, in that order. Rebecca never entirely recovered her health after that last pregnancy. Ella stepped in at that point, to take over the day-to-day household chores for father and siblings.

All the children of The Grand House attended local Catholic schools. St James's at Spring Hill was preferred for the boys. The Christian Brothers appeared to have been ruthless taskmasters. More than once, Rebecca trotted to the school to give them a good dressing down: she considered the punishments meted out were too severe. The O'Shea boys next door and the O'Rourke children up the road were also classmates of Ella's brothers and sister. My mother once confided she never enjoyed school (leading me to ponder if likes and dislikes could be inherited).

Rebecca was an adamant ex-Jewess: children should adhere to the teachings of the Church. This meant they rarely missed Mass and Communion on Sunday.

Paddy would rarely have been up to the task.

From all accounts, growing up during the Depression in that part of Brisbane despite the shortage of material possessions was equal to all the blind fun of Cork. This became especially so after the Crystal Palace cinema opened in 1921. The original theatre bears little resemblance to the one that closed its doors for the last time in 1999. In 1921, there was an impressively arched entry-foyer facing Gympie Road. Peculiarly enough, there was no roof over the first few rows of seats, which must have made viewing invigorating when it rained.

The exposed seats at the front were wooden stools. One had to be relatively affluent to move out of the elements and into the canvas seats. On Saturday arvo, all the neighbourhood kids were at the flicks catching up on the continuing adventures of *Scotty the Scout* (a popular silent serial). On Wednesday nights the children of The Grand House would roll up with their mother for the weekly movie, featuring titles like *Emily the Ghost*.

The annual excursion to Cribb Island was also a big deal. Before this epic journey could be undertaken, Rebecca would insist Paddy spruce up his T-Model with its regulation green paint. As they set out, Rebecca would proudly sit up the front with Paddy. A wicker chair was temporarily installed on the back tray specifically for the comfort of Paddy's mother, who joined them most years until she died.

A wooden bench was subsequently fixed onto the back tray for Paddy and Rebecca's offspring to be arranged neatly in a row. If some of Paddy's nieces came along, they roosted along the tray and dangled their legs over the side (looking all very *Beverly Hillbillies*). Rebecca's good friend Mrs. O'Shea and her family always took their holiday at the same time. Lacking anything quite so grand as a T-Model, they nevertheless made the trip as regularly in their horse and cart.

There were certain sanctified rituals associated with the pilgrimage to Cribb Island. The way was enshrined with pit stops - one being at The Prince of Wales Hotel, at Nundah. It was visited when approaching from either direction. At this point, whilst the respective carriages and occupants waited under the spreading fig outside, Paddy and Mr. O'Shea would go in for a cleansing ale.

When Ella reached fourteen, Paddy secured her a job sorting tobacco at the Dalgety factory in Milton, near to the 4X brewery today. The brewery was prominent on the skyline even back then. Ella recalls that, whenever possible, Paddy would time his collections and deliveries at Dalgety's to coincide with the daily freebie at the brewery: at certain hours they offered a traditional glass of beer, gratis, to workers in the area.

As an employed girl, Ella cheerfully gave half her salary to her mother and usually set aside a shilling for a flutter on the horses. The racetrack at Kedron Park had closed. Alternative venues were at Albion Park and Eagle Farm.

Benjamin was also earning his keep, resourcefully hiring a horse and cart from Kenny Brothers in Butterfield Street, for five shillings a week. He filled the cart with fruit and veg at the markets in Roma Street, then hawked the produce door to door. He also had a weekend job at the nearby bakery, operated by Paddy's cousins.

Paddy became increasingly stubborn in his ways, relative to the deterioration of Rebecca's health. She must have been particularly crisis ridden the day Ella and Cecelia discovered her sitting at the kitchen table with a carving knife. She had been contemplating slashing her wrists. Mercifully, she was persuaded to put down the knife on the promise of a bottle of wine. This she promptly skulled without pausing for breath. Considering her teetotal past, the effect was to part the seas for a great exodus of hysteria.

Around this time, the first of a series of tragedies struck The Grand House. It started late one Sunday morning, when Benjamin came home from his shift at the bakery. He decided to snatch a few zeds, before heading to Downey Park for an afternoon cricket match with the neighbourhood lads.

Rebecca was in two minds about disturbing her son from his sound sleep at the time specified. Of course, such hesitation was short-lived. After all, she would do absolutely anything her darling first-born boy requested.

Because it was a typically sultry summer afternoon in Brisbane: after the game, most kids opted for a dip in a popular waterhole known as Pebbly Bottom. Benjamin and his mates jumped in enthusiastically. Following a short splash and frolic they emerged one by one from the creek. When Benjamin was nowhere to be seen, a couple of mates went back to the waterhole to see if he was still there.

One of them kicked a submerged object with his foot. Blood rose to the surface. They discovered Benjamin's lifeless body. He had dived in the shallows and broken his neck. Benjamin was barely out of his teens when he was buried next to his biological father at Toowong Cemetery. A recent photo of him wearing his baggy cricket cap was enlarged and framed. It was hung on the dining-room wall at The Grand House, not far from the photo of his mother, Rebecca. Oddly enough, their ages would have been similar when each photo was taken.

Not too long after this tragedy, Rebecca succumbed to her illness. Ella rose from apprentice to *chief cook and bottle-washer* at The Grand House.

# Chapter Eight

By the time Rebecca passed away, Ella's younger sister, Cecelia had been working for some time at a clothing factory in all the hustle and bustle of Roma Street. In those days, Roma Street doubled as the site of Brisbane's fruit-and-veg markets.

Cecelia once confided she was so nervous on her first day at work, she put her shoes on the wrong feet. She failed to notice until after lunch. She, too, was positively desperate to succeed in the workforce having loathed every minute spent at St. Columba's School. Mercifully, she mastered the skills of her new tailoring craft quickly.

Ella's brother, Jack found employment at the Perkins' soft-drink factory just up the road from The Grand House. Not, however, without some incident. Within no time at all, he lost a finger from his right hand in a machinery accident.

Increased family obligations didn't prevent Ella from enjoying some degree of social life. The Kangaroo Point Cycle Club and the Trocadero Dance Hall at South Brisbane were popular. Patrons, incidentally, still included Mickey O'Rourke's children. Everyone continued to patronise an all-time favorite: the Crystal Palace, which had undergone some radical changes since it first opened. Now there was a roof over the entire theatre and the wooden stools were nowhere to be seen. The canvas seats had been relegated to the front, cheap section, whilst the back rows now sported the latest in luxury, padded chairs.

Despite sage admonitions from elderly generations today, the track record of kids in the years between the First and Second World Wars was no shining example. Rival gangs based on territories are hardly a novel phenomenon. In the thirties they were an integral part of youth culture. Young men from around The Grand House district belonged to the Rosemount clique. These would lock horns with a crowd from Newstead. Such confrontations usually took place near the showgrounds.

I'm also led to believe there was a particularly nasty bunch called The Razor Gang, whose menace sullied the Valley's reputation. Similar groups posed a potentially lethal threat to unwary night-walkers, throughout Paddington and South Brisbane. Fiftybob's boys, Martin and Jack were prominent in the Rosemount group.

It seems Fiftybob was financially better off than his younger brother. Fergus exhibited some suspiciously self-serving traits; *entrepreneurial* qualities of the kind celebrated in corporate boardrooms. Perhaps this is why he was a tad more affluent than Paddy. Whatever the source, he sent his boys to the more acclaimed St Joseph's College at Gregory Terrace. His boys were driving motor vehicles by their late teens. Unfortunately, the younger of the two, Jack wrote himself off in his car at Albion, one Saturday night. *Jack* was proving a bad omen, if there's anything in a name.

On another momentous Saturday night, Ella attended a dance held by the Brisbane Restricted Sailing Club. She went with a work colleague, Rose Murphy, whose brother, Declan was a keen sailor and club member. At the dance, Ella was introduced to Claude, an old school chum of Declan Murphy's.

It just so happened that Claude's father was president of the club. Claude's and Declan Murphy's parents were neighbours. The two boys had grown up together in Stratton Street, even attending St. Patrick's and St. James's schools together.

Ella wasn't impressed with Claude on their first encounter. She held the sole reservation that his dancing was praiseworthy. Somehow, he seemed a bit of a know-all; she was hardly surprised to learn his nickname was 'Professor.' Nevertheless, she thought she would grant him one more opportunity to redeem himself - since he contacted her a few days later to persuade her to the pictures. (She always said she wasn't fussy.)

It didn't take long for her feelings about him to change. Before too long they were discussing marriage. This brought on quite a dilemma for Ella. Claude was keen to set up house around New Farm. She was heartily reluctant to leave The Grand House, where father and siblings depended on her. After all, her youngest brother, Fergus was just a schoolboy who had recently suffered the trauma of losing his mother. Ella prickled with anxious concern for his prospects - leaving him at that tender age to contend with their father, Paddy.

When Paddy realised where the relationship between his daughter and this young man was heading, he resolved on a strategy of his own.

At this point, Paddy swore to Ella:

*If she stayed at The Grand House: he would leave it to her when he died.*

# Chapter Nine

Early in 1939, Ella and Claude married at St. Patrick's Church in the Valley. For the auspicious occasion, Ella wore a cream, satin dress with a lace overcoat, which had been run up for her by Mrs. O'Shea next door. She told me she wore that dress for *best* many years after. Immediately following the wedding, without so much as a hint of a honeymoon they moved into the main bedroom of The Grand House. That room, when last jointly occupied had been Rebecca's and Paddy's.

Paddy relocated to the front bedroom off the hallway. The houseguest remained ensconced in the room off the dining area, which everyone agreed was the best bedroom despite being the smallest. (It was the only bedroom with the warm morning sun, whilst being sheltered by the verandah from intense afternoon rays.)

I can only second-guess the intricacies of the relationship that existed many years before I appeared, and which doubtless permeated every hanging innuendo. From what I gather, a grudging acceptance between Paddy and his son-in-law became the status quo. Paddy considered The Grand House his domain. This short-arsed, half-baked pommie know-all was nothing more than an intruder.

Claude had by far the softer nature of the two men. There again, Paddy made most men look a little marshmallowy. Claude was even prone to cry over a sad song without having to be drunk! At least a healthy friendship developed between Claude and the houseguest, as well as with Ella's younger brothers and sister.

Claude moved out of his dapper, English-born father's home in Stratton Street, Newstead, to be with his new wife at The Grand House. Claude's parents, his younger brother and maternal grandmother occupied a modest rented house next to the Horitz soft-drink factory. She had grudgingly shifted from Charters Towers after her husband's death. Ella describes her mother-in-law's mother as a drunken, abusive Irishwoman (which she shortened to *that Irishwoman* when vexed).

She felt her bias was justified after having witnessed an incident involving on the one hand, an exceedingly affable Aboriginal lady. She lived with her white husband and children in a house next to Ella's in-laws, in Stratton Street. Their dwelling was on the empty side of sparse: the couple was evidently floundering in the financial slurries. This didn't deter the indigenous woman from finding it in her heart to go to the expense of presenting each of her neighbours with a Christmas box of beautifully wrapped soap.

This particular year, Ella's grandmother-in-law's reaction to this kind gesture was unexpected, astonishing and obviously alcohol induced. The old soak accused the poor unsuspecting gift-bearer of intimating that she needed a wash. (Well, everyone else thought she did.) To this day, Ella insists a gift of soap is the most sarcastic manner imaginable of critiquing a lady's imperfections.

The Stratton Street dwellers - Ella's in-law territory - were predominantly Anglo-Irish. Collectively speaking, they were given to eccentric behaviour, to put it delicately. One family, who wore the Irish hallmark with their home directly opposite, was unusually large (numerically, not physically. In fact, my mother was quite adamant about the limited stature vis-à-vis of the man of the house. I thought this a bit rich coming from someone of garden-gnome proportions herself.)

Regardless, the story goes that this vertically challenged Irishman would regularly quaff himself silly at the Waterloo Hotel, at the end of the street. This, in full awareness of the consequences: he would have to face the wrath of his voluminous, self-appointed better half waiting like the female red-back, at home.

Stumbling and grappling, he would heave his tun to the top of the stairs where his wife lurked in readiness to seize him by the scruff of the neck, grab the top of his pants and hurl him back down again. Ella and the Old Man would regularly amuse themselves watching this unfold. It was like Saturday afternoon pantomime, visiting Claude's parents' house.

Incidentally, the Old Man is my father. Naturally, this isn't the name I used to address him when a child. It is, however, the epithet chosen most readily by his children these days.

Going back for a moment to the day of their wedding, Ella and Claude couldn't afford a professional photographer. Even with their Kodak Box Brownie working overtime in the hands of friends and relatives, they produced no fitting wedding photo. On their first anniversary, they determined to rectify the situation by staging the event for posterity. Their wedding FX photo was enlarged, framed then placed on the wall at The Grand House near Rebecca's and Benjamin's.

During that first year of wedded bliss, the Old Man placed a deposit on a sumptuous, waist-length, rabbit-fur coat for his new wife.

This was intended as a *sort-of* belated wedding gift. Ella looks quite some dapper dame, drenched in fur on the wall photo.

But surely, this following incident must have rung alarm bells for her? Whilst the Old Man forked out the initial down payment, Ella had to outlay all subsequent instalments until the coat was hers. Luckily she continued to work at Dalgety's after she married. In fact, she sometimes earned more than her husband. In those days the basic male wage was four pounds, six shillings a week. Ella could earn five pounds or more at the tobacco factory, where they paid by the amount sorted not the hours worked.

Ella wasn't frightened of hard work. No-one would argue *she* needed to go to an art gallery to see a sunrise. On the contrary, on any given day Ella was out of bed before *sparrow fart* (one of Paddy's favoured terms). Once up and doing, she operated at nineteen-to-the-dozen all day before collapsing into the cot. With such a healthy combined income during those early days of married life, they even succeeded in putting aside a small nest egg.

In his defence, the Old Man's handy-work saved them a bob or two. He was an extremely talented carpenter. However, everything he constructed was so solid and faithfully reinforced, once the item had been instated, the building would have to be knocked down to relocate it. He constructed the one and only bedroom suite they ever possessed. Its eccentric components included a massively ornate wardrobe, *Hers,* and a shrunken, ordinary version, *His.* There was also a duchesse and double bed-head. The finished product looked stylish and immaculate, like a pricey store-bought piece, although the sombre stain lent it a little too much gravity.

Later, as the family expanded, he created a kitchen table I can only imagine was inspired by Da Vinci's 'The Last Supper': its dimensions were so transcendent. It certainly transcended any available kitchen space. It had to be pushed up against the wall when not in use to create a minimal passage around the kitchen. Meal times regularly demanded a labour-force of at least two each end to lift it out. As an accompaniment to the acreage of table, he assembled a hardwood form-bench on which we children sat for meals. It, too, was built to resist just about anything on the Richter scale.

I couldn't do justice to the catalogue of his handiwork without including at least one glossy photo of this unique single bed. It was twice as long as a standard single and, naturally, constructed from solidly reinforced hardwood. You cannot imagine how heavy it was! It was intended to sleep two, end-to-end, with feet touching in the middle. I can only suppose mum must have become quietly proficient in sheet collage.

Another glossy close-up from his *custom* catalogue features the many wooden trucks and pull-along toys he made as Christmas presents for the boys. I can still hear the swinging horse - suspended from rafters under the front verandah - neighing creakily in high winds. That's the affectionate remainder of a fast-fading text of memories called *My Father*.

# Chapter Ten

Late in 1939, Claude and Ella's first child was delivered in the spanking new Royal Women's Hospital. Ella had turned up to the official opening of this impressive building several months earlier. The event was celebrated with the release of hundreds of white doves from the top floor. The skyline of the general hospital was on the rise. I'm led to believe this was thanks to Golden Casket ticket sales. That being the case, mum's Casket flutters must have financed at least one ward.

My entire childhood is polka-dotted with memories of her excitedly scouring the Casket draw. She survived on the vain hope of winning that illusive prize, which would come to her like a golden T-Model from the sky and rescue her from the cycle of poverty (which had well and truly trapped her by the time I came along).

Anyway, back to their baby. She was a pretty, dark-haired, green-eyed girl they called Patrice, in honour of her grandfather, Patrick. When you come from Irish stock, you never know if a ginger-haired child will abruptly spring from the family gene pool. Ginger or black occurs due to an allelomorphic gene; meaning one colour-gene has two forms. (So, the appearance of a redhead doesn't necessitate desperate inquisitions as to who the real father was.)

Ella was hopeful to avoid the ginger type. Because Rebecca's lastborn son displayed a shock of coppery curls soon after birth, Ella was wary of the same fate befalling hers. My mother once confided one of the first things she checked, after verifying the obvious items were intact, was the colour of her newborn baby's hair.

Ella and Claude were so rapt with their new daughter, they took her along for all to admire at the fanfare opening of Cloudland Ballroom. They were there, too, proudly pushing the pram with bonny baby across the Story Bridge when it was declared operational.

Not long after Patrice entered the picture, at Claude's behest, they invested in an upright piano for the princely sum of ten pounds. The money was likely to have come from their nest egg. I presume the decision to outlay such a significant amount on a luxury item would not have been taken lightly.

The ten-pound price tag was a bargain stemming from tragedy. The piano belonged to one of the first Australian casualties of the war in

Europe. His parents, who lived near The Grand House, could no longer bear his deathly silent memento around the home. So they were prepared to let it go for an elegy.

Up till this point, the Old Man had never experienced a piano lesson, yet he could recreate almost any tune after hearing it a few times. Nanny was a reasonable pianist so perhaps he had acquired the aptitude from her. Further down the track he did take a few classes at a music college in Brisbane. This equipped him to read sheet music. The advent of the piano ushered in an era of wonderful singsong gatherings at The Grand House for Ella, Claude, family and friends alike.

The war continued unabated in Europe. Ella's brother, Jack was dead keen to join the airforce. As long as Jack remained under recruitment age, Paddy steadfastly refused to sign permission for him to enlist. I don't know whether he was chiefly motivated by fear of losing his son or by his outright loathing of English royalty. Paddy made it perfectly clear to all and sundry from the outset of war: he had no intention of fighting for King and Country.

One time, whilst making his way through the Valley, he was handed a white feather. (Given to civilian men of fighting age who exhibited no visible excuse for being out of uniform.) Paddy didn't mince his words as he promptly handed it back, advising the gift-bearer to 'Stick it up your arse!'

Ella was relieved to learn her husband wouldn't be required for active service. His work at the cheese factory in South Brisbane was construed vital for supplying the troops.

As Japan's imperial front edged ever nearer, two enormous fuel-tanks were positioned just up the road from The Grand House. The chosen location for these mammoths was an old quarry. The fuel-tanks were camouflaged as tennis courts for the duration of the war. Considering the highly combustible nature of their contents, those in the immediate vicinity of Rosemount and Swan Hill lived in constant apprehension. The conflagration would have extended over quite a few neighbourhoods had they been bombed.

When that grim chapter was finally concluded, the tanks stayed on as a monumental reminder of yet another chilling episode in twentieth-century history - prehistoric states of mind poised to rise again like the heads of interred warriors. They remained landmarks in Swan Hill for thirty years or more. Only towards the end of the century were they removed and the site taken by a variety of Homemaker Stores including Freedom Furniture.

By 1941, Jack was old enough to join the fray without his father's permission. He let few days slip before signing up with the army. After undertaking basic training, he was promptly given his marching orders towards Rabaul, in September that year.

The Old Man was all the family at South Brisbane station as the young soldier boarded the northbound train, on the first leg of his voyage to New Guinea. The houseguest had been called up for work on the wharf that morning. Ella felt it would be too distressing for Patrice to see her mother so upset (as would have been the case if she had gone all the way to the station). Instead, she said good-bye to her brother at The Grand House as he enthusiastically departed.

Jack looked so proud of himself in his army uniform.

Paddy's stubborn nature was the only obstacle to his being there, to bid his son adieu. He never wanted his boy to enlist. They were still embroiled in an argument about it when Jack departed on his first tour of duty.

Ella received several heavily censored letters from Jack between September and November. He wrote of catching malaria and his eagerness to receive some news about the family. In one such correspondence, he enclosed a snapshot of himself in uniform taken at Chinatown, Rabaul. Ella wrote to him every week without fail, about happenings on the home front. This included news that he would soon be an uncle, again. Ever hopeful of keeping his spirits up, she suggested he might like to be the godfather to his new niece or nephew once he returned.

By early December, the letters from Jack stopped. At this point, Ella began a ritual of calling into the department in Brisbane where they kept records of enlisted men. Every visit ended in disappointment and frustration. On one occasion, she was informed that her brother's records, along with those of many others had been misplaced. It happened during a security precaution, effected when a Japanese invasion seemed imminent. Jack was officially listed as *missing in action* on the 1$^{st}$ of July 1942.

Ella had the snapshot from Rabaul enlarged and framed. She placed it on the wall next to the photos of Rebecca and Benjamin. Sometime later, she received a parcel. It contained every letter she had written to her brother. Not one had been opened. They were all marked, *Address Unknown.*

# Chapter Eleven

On the fourth of July 1942, four days after Jack was officially listed as missing, Ella and Claude's second child was born. The baby was given the name Claude after his father. He soon became known as Little Claude. Little Claude was his mother's pride and joy. Ella boasted about the number who stopped in the street to comment how beautiful her baby was with olive skin, dark hair and brown eyes. His swarthy features were a spitting image of the young soldier whose youth was now enshrined in a black-and-white photo on the wall.

As lovely as he was to look at, from all reports he was a bugger of a baby. He slept so little Ella even resorted to putting a nip of brandy in his water at times. When he was awake, almost all the time, he would never let mum out of his sight. This situation leads me to the story of Mrs. Grey.

For as long as I can remember, there had been a fibro duplex next to The Grand House. My mother recalls Rebecca frequently urging Paddy to buy that little corner block, so she could set up a shop. That never happened. Someone else acquired the land and built the fibro duplex. The flats saw a procession of tenants over ensuing years, many of whom became friends with Grand House residents.

One such was an ever so kind lady called Mrs. Grey. Mrs. Grey went out of her way to help. Ella was evidently needy, having her hands full with two small children, a belligerent old father and a husband who drank more than was prudent, considering his responsibilities.

If Ella needed to duck away on an errand, Mrs. Grey would be only too happy to keep an eye on the children. *Ducking* anywhere proved quite a challenge for Ella who had no end of trouble with her clinging son. Ella would take Patrice and Little Claude to Mrs. Grey's, on the pretext of a cuppa. As soon as Little Claude was preoccupied with Mrs. Grey fussing over him, Ella would sneak down the steps, then make a dash up the hill towards the tram-stop. Inevitably, before she gained so much as a few tiptoe-holds along the footpath, Little Claude would be wailing at her from Mrs. Grey's window at such volume, cats could be seen scattering over fences.

The Grand House was well serviced by trams by the time the forties were in full swing. Having access to regular public transport was a real bonus. Paddy had long since dispensed with the T-Model in the unusual manner described earlier. Now he jumped on the tram to travel to his packer's job at the cheese factory. (The position no doubt secured by his son-in-law.)

Claude's days at that factory were, by now, drawing to a close. This was largely due to a suggestion made by a work mate. His plan was to start a business. The Old Man, after some deliberation decided the venture was too risky. His colleague pushed ahead to found what is now one of Brisbane's oldest and most successful catering companies.

That turn of events set the Old Man earnestly searching for ways to improve his economic prospects, without the vulnerability of self-employment. Next thing you knew, he was taking up the houseguest's offer to put his name down for the wharf.

Waterside-worker positions were so sought after; they weren't advertised in any conventional way. It was invariably nepotism that opened the door. Mind you, they worked damn hard for their money before mechanisation and containers, when lifting was carried out manually. One man could spend up to eight hours in the bowels of the ship, in freezing conditions hauling heavy crates. On the positive side, the money was great, especially for midnights or weekends. Not forgetting an added bonus - the odd item accidentally dropping into your Gladstone bag out of a broken crate.

By the time the Old Man commenced as a waterside worker, Ella's young ginger-haired brother, Fergus was also dutifully turning the treadmill of workaday regimes. His career started at the nearby grocery store on the recommendation of one of the O'Shea family (still Grand House neighbours). From there, he moved to employment at a prominent Roma Street merchant, close to Cecilia's workplace at the clothing factory. Braving all disdain from his father, he also took to playing Australian Rules for Windsor Club. (Paddy scornfully described the game as *aerial ping-pong*.)

Windsor Club's home ground in those days was at Albion. The Sunday matches were at Perry Park, where admission was a silver coin. Young ginger-haired Fergus must have played with Windsor Football Club for a fair while.

I have vague recollections of the shortcut to Perry Park, through the Mayne railway yards. I would nervously scurry across tracks tangled like strewn spaghetti. Little Claude's warning about junctions where crisscross lines can instantly change by remote control had me jumping up and down like a terrified mouse. I kept getting an image of my foot being trapped and, as I struggle to free myself, a speeding train approaches. This scenario spooked me so often (like a scene from Alfred Hitchcock) I suspected it must be a premonition.

I'm convinced having older brothers can permanently scar your childhood.

Fergus wore number 16 on his jersey. This number became indelibly imprinted on Ella's mind after a particular Sunday match. One of her tasks was to wash his jersey. Before she could do this, the number had to be removed to prevent shrinkage. In a typical morning-rush situation, she sewed the numbers on upside down. Her error was humiliatingly brought to her attention when her brother ran onto the field.

'Who's that ginger-haired bloke wearing ninety one?' yelled a voice from the crowd.

One of Fergus's teammates, playing with Windsor Australian Rules Club, was Mickey O'Rourke's son, Shamus. These two families had by now been friends for many years. With haunting synchronicity, Mickey's wife also died leaving the eldest daughter, Grace, to raise the family. In her case, the youngest was a baby of two. Those were busy days for both Ella and Grace. Life was to become even more hectic for Ella when she realised a third baby was due, in November of 1945.

Regrettably, before that infant was to make its entrance another soul was to depart. The houseguest was nearing retirement age when he stepped off a tram and into the path of an oncoming vehicle, at the stop just behind The Grand House. He had the uncertain distinction of becoming the first victim from The Grand House on that ominous section of the Gympie Road.

# Chapter Twelve

Baby number three, Russell, was born without a hint of ginger hair. He was named in honour of the houseguest, who was killed a few weeks earlier. Ella certainly had her hands full now, and Little Claude's antics didn't help matters one bit. She vividly recalls walking up and down the hallway in an effort to settle the new baby, with Little Claude hanging onto her skirt all the while.

Baby Russell became rather attached to Paddy, while the latter was recuperating from a broken leg. Uncannily, that accident occurred not long after the houseguest was killed and in the same manner. He, too, was disembarking from a tram along that treacherous stretch of Gympie Road at the back of The Grand House. Paddy was in the company of Mickey O'Rourke and didn't fare as badly as his old school chum from Gympie. Perhaps there's something in the saying that *god protects drunks and babies*! Both he and Mickey were three sheets to the wind when the incident occurred.

Mickey's brother was prominent in legal circles at the time, which worked to Paddy's advantage. He was able to secure a reasonable compensation payoff from the driver. Thus, he was able to convalesce for several months, mostly in the old wicker-chair under the mango tree in the backyard with baby Russell. Russell first learned to stand by pulling himself up on his grandfather's wicker chair. Almost as soon as he could walk, Paddy had the toddler catching and throwing a ball. He was convinced this boy would be the best five-eighth in Queensland.

Speaking of growing up, by now Patrice was a student at Ella's and Cecelia's old school. She was developing into a delightfully sociable child, eager to spend weekends at her grandparents' house in Stratton Street. So far, Little Claude couldn't be coaxed into flying the nest for a similar adventure. And young Russell would bolt to his mother's side, every time granddad arrived to surprise the young fellow with his comical *Bulla Bulla* greeting.

Around this time, Cecelia vacated The Grand House. Unlike her sister, Cecelia never displayed any real aptitude, or perhaps it was regard for cooking and keeping house. This is possibly why she decided to board with Mrs. Wren. Of course, another provocation could have been the crowded and complicated living conditions at The Grand

House. Regardless, she was a single girl with a steady income and that afforded the luxury of paying someone to fuss over her.

Mrs. Wren willingly provided a room in her little nest. She was a widow with a married son in Rockhampton and a bachelor, John, residing. The arrangement with Cecelia appeared to suit all three. Cecelia and John cultivated a relationship of a sort, which lasted many years despite remaining platonic to all appearances. John was a jovial gentle-giant who drove equally large tip-trucks for a living.

Before long, Mrs. Wren was dressmaking for her star boarder. The three took annual holidays to Rockhampton, where they stayed with John's brother and his family. The threesome were also regulars at Saturday's race meetings.

Ella, too, loved an excursion to the races, though three young children rigorously restricted her. She determined to make the effort on the festive day of Eagle Farm's re-opening. (It had been closed for most of the war years, to house American troops.) Claude and his old school chum, Declan Murphy escorted Ella to 'the Flat'.

The Flat, which was accessed by crossing the racetrack to the middle-oval, was the domain of the battler punter. The moderate two and six entry fee made it attractive for the financially affrighted.

Before continuing the story of *the three musketeers*, I should share Ella's capricious manner of picking a winner. Her selections were based on a whim, a colour, last night's dream or a name reminiscent of someone or any thing. As she pondered and patiently waited for ethereal inspiration for investing her meagre kitty, a man brushed against her and whispered 'number eleven.'

This was the omen she had been hoping for. She immediately bet on the nose of number eleven in the next race. To the amazement of her sceptical companions, the horse romped home to pay a handsome dividend. When questioned about her selection of such a rank outsider from the field of favourites, she pointed to her mystery source in the crowd. Declan and Claude were speechless. It turned out her phantom tipster was a known identity around the racetrack who was completely deaf and mute.

Ella and Claude put on a party at The Grand House that evening. Ella sang her little heart out at the piano all night long.

# Chapter Thirteen

In January 1947, sandy-haired baby Royce arrived. Not being a robust child he demanded a considerable measure of Ella's attention. Apart from childbirth, poor Ella hadn't spent so much as a night away from The Grand House. The last time being back in the good old days, when Paddy's entourage would undertake the annual pilgrimage to Cribb Island in the T-Model.

She was understandably excited therefore, at the prospect of a camping holiday down to Wellington Point. Her husband planned it for her and the children, in the joint company of a work-mate and his tribe. Unfortunately, the junket didn't live up to Ella's expectations. She described it as an absolute wash out.

Not only did it rain for the entire week, the Old Man and his colleague spending every day in the pub really threw a wet blanket over the occasion. This left the little ladies and their offspring to entertain each other. The two women strained to be amicable, while the kids fought as though terminal delinquency had set in.

I'm only relating this incident because out of it, the great wooden boat appeared.

The Old Man's love of water went back to well before the time he sailed into Ella's life. He and Declan Murphy were crew on a yacht called Rhythm. I recall seeing a photo of it somewhere around The Grand House when young. I can still visualise a sleek craft under full sail, emblazoned with a musical note (a crotchet). That 18 foot sharpie must have won its fair share of races. I say this because several tarnished trophy cups became receptacles for oddments (drawing pins, bits of jigsaw puzzle).

Considering his close connection to the sea, it was hardly surprising he failed to resist temptation on spying a derelict craft going for next to nothing at Wellington Point. A mate towed it by water, as far as the bend in the creek, at the end of the street. It was then a labour-intensive effort of pyramid-building proportions to transport it the remaining distance to its resting-place beside The Grand House.

The chore took the best part of the day and it exhausted considerable manpower. They had devised a tortuous roll-and-lift technique involving logs. Once in place, it remained in a perpetual state of renovation for years after I entered the picture.

Incidentally, I became baby number five (in case you have lost count) towards the end of '49. By then, Little Claude had embarked on his journey through the Catholic education system, in which Patrice was already established. Still on the sideboard at The Grand House today is a delightful photo of Patrice and Little Claude at a school fancy-dress ball. Patrice went as a fairy and Little Claude as an elf. I doubt if he would have been more than six when that moment was captured. (I also doubt he would appreciate it being on general view.)

My impending arrival did nothing to stymie Ella's gambling on the horses. I was born on Caulfield Cup day. She still managed to bet on Comic Court somewhere between the onset of labour and admission to The Royal Women's Hospital. Placing a bet from The Grand House never posed a major problem. This was despite the fact that the in-house electric telephone and TAB were both way into the future. Not only were houses pampered by two postal deliveries each weekday, one on Saturday; there was the dubious bounty of a weekly SP-bookie service.

Rain, hail, sleet, snow or shine the bookie, cleverly disguised as a tradesman, invariably came through to collect bets on Friday and settle up on Sunday. Before I became worldly wise, I was perplexed a workman could call so often with no visible improvement around the decrepit old place. Of course at that age, I almost literally *had* come down in the last shower.

I was born on a Saturday morning (I can't remember if it was raining or not). As they wheeled Ella into the ward that afternoon, she was desperately grimacing, mustering all her telepathic energy to will Comic Court to victory.

The horse fell over!

Something must have broken her concentration.

That wasn't the end of the Comic Court saga by a long stretch. Ella had her money on his nose again, as he moved between the barriers to start the 1950 Melbourne Cup.

Mrs. Grey stuck her head out the window of the duplex next door, when the first horse crossed the line in the big race.

'Did you back it today, Ella?' she screeched.

She won a bounteous sum. She was also becoming increasingly canny: when informing the Old Man of her good fortune, she downplayed the amount. Covert kitty in hand, she promptly purchased Christmas presents for the kids and new linoleum for the kitchen.

# Chapter Fourteen

Linoleum, or lino as we knew it was synonymous with growing up mid-century before wall-to-wall carpet took pride of place. Actually, the product we trod underfoot at The Grand House was a still cheaper and thinner variety called congolium. It was a novel event whenever a new roll was unfurled in the old dwelling. There was lino on virtually every floor, except the verandah, which remained bare-boarded.

Ella had a bit of *a thing* about mats. The upshot was a proliferation of little door slips and a mile-long hall-runner from backdoor to front. Fresh lino was destined for the kitchen, being the high-traffic area. Apart from formal gatherings, such as Christmas and birthdays, every mealtime was in the kitchen. It would be all hands on deck to shift heavy items or, to be specific, the monumental table. The old lino would then be carefully lifted to facilitate recycling to other parts of the house. This recycling process turned the bedroom floors into variegated lino patchwork. The old covering would be pulled back to reveal layers of newspaper underlay.

There was no shortage of newsprint in those days. The Courier hit the streets every Monday through Saturday. Two rival Sunday tabloids vied to capitalise on the most primal of urges by the tenor of their headlines. On street corners paperboys earned a pittance spruiking, *'Tele! Tele! Get your Tele!'* as they flogged the early and late edition of that now defunct rag.

Revisiting the past in old newsprint provided an hilarious diversion from the chore of laying lino. Old advertisements were particularly intriguing. Finney Isles, Allan & Stark and McDonnell & East all ran broadsheet spreads, highlighting the hottest in new apparel - fashionable topcoats for ladies and smart double-breasted pinstriped suits with cuffed trousers for the man. Strewn amongst the old newspapers could be found pages from old Pix, People and Post magazines (the Old Man's favourite reads). They attracted a different style of advertising. We guffawed at the purported medicinal benefits of the cola tonic drink, guaranteed to relieve fatigue. The myriad of mail-order enticements was overwhelming. Ever prominent was a bodybuilding course, a failsafe way for the seven-stone weakling never again to have sand kicked in his eyes by the bigger guys. (I had never really been party to these sand-kicking rituals at the beach. It always struck me as flawed reasoning when, after all, the little guys could simply wear larger sunglasses.) Assorted ointments and salves could cure any conceivable dilemma from baldness to unsightly hair.

Eventually the floorboards would be swept for fresh papers to be laid, in readiness for the bright new pattern. Ella always cut and laid the lino herself using her unique tools of trade. These included a sharp blade from any source and any old piece of wood she could lay her hands on, for a straight edge. The result might not always have borne close scrutiny but neither did much else around the place in those days.

The Grand House was exhibiting palpable proof of more than twenty-five years of wear and tear with no serious expenditure on maintenance. The Old Man had thrown in the towel on bothering awhile back. This, I suspect, was under duress. Every time he attempted home improvements, Paddy felt compelled to challenge his authority to do so.

A case in point, there were the logs, which I assumed were a legacy of dry docking the boat some time ago. The Old Man had a resourceful notion to terrace a section of the backyard with these (where the land sloped too severely to cut with a hand-mower). Having successfully completed this much landscaping, he felt gratified by his able contribution.

That feeling was to be short-lived, when Paddy promptly transferred the logs to another spot.

In this environment, it was hardly surprising the Old Man's enthusiasm for such activities waned, in direct proportion to a rise in pub time away from the place.

# Chapter Fifteen

I was christened in the traditional way with Uncle Fergus as godfather and a family friend who worked with him, as godmother. My godmother, with her delightful Irish name of Irene was a single lady. Throughout my entire childhood she never let my birthday pass without sending a card containing a ten-shilling note. Thank-you Irene, may your gracious caring be a never-forgotten standard!

The year of my birth was significant for Fergus in more ways than one. Not only was he blessed with the singular distinction of being my godfather, he was in the undefeated premiership team at Windsor Football Club. What a double!

As a matter of fact, there was a great deal happening in Fergus's life. He had been nurturing the affections of a young lady whose family lived at Albion. Around this time they tied the knot and he vacated The Grand House. On my sideboard, I keep a framed snapshot of Ella taken at Fergus's wedding, in which she holds a toddler I barely recognise as me.

Their first son, Little Fergus was born without ginger hair, in November '51. The very same day, Patrice celebrated her twelfth birthday. A second son, Phillip, also sans carrot top entered the picture a couple of years later.

While these events were unfolding, Fergus was a malcontent at Foley Bros. His dissatisfaction had him contemplating sundry career options, even fireman. That was until his brother-in-law, Claude intimated the possibility of securing him a position on the wharf. My uncle was keen on the idea. Unfortunately, *keen* didn't describe the reaction of his wife. She held a low opinion of waterside workers and resisted her husband's attempts to number among them.

When the couple first married, she might not have held such a rigorously judgmental view. However, in the intervening period a miraculous event happened in her life. She followed a flock to find herself in the midst of a Billy Graham congregation at the Exhibition Grounds. That day she saw the light. With her new-found religious pique, she didn't care to have her husband associating with the likes of waterside workers (with their reputation for questionable practices).

The Old Man put Fergus's name down anyway, not seriously considering anything would come of it. Vacancies on the wharf were as scarce as hens' teeth.

Then, Hallelujah! To everyone's surprise, Fergus's number came up.

Then came the sticky quandary of how to broach the matter with his holier half. I wouldn't be at all surprised if he resorted to Black Magic (chocolates, of course). A bouquet of blooms from the nearby Roma Street markets might also have come into play. He needed all the ammunition he could muster for this ambush. Once he had promised religiously to resist any temptation to deviate from the straight and narrow path of righteousness, Fergus was finally permitted to join the Waterside Workers Federation.

As with most in the rudimentary stages of married life, especially with two small offspring in tow, it was a financial nightmare. In the early days, their mode of transport was an old truck, which they later upgraded to a modest VW. My aunt being somewhat capacious, rump-wise, often made my mind boggle (when they left The Grand House after a visit) as to how all that flesh squeezed down into such a confined space.

For awhile, they thrived in a rudimentary one-room cabin on small acreage at Mount Cotton, on Brisbane's south side. In those days it was virgin bushland with little sign of development. I imagine they intended to add to the structure as they earned more. I daresay that part of the bush is considerably less *virgin* today.

During this period, my uncle had been failing to resist temptation at the wharf. His biggest hurdle wasn't smuggling it out of the wharves but in explaining the origin of his booty when he arrived home. He found it easier to stash the items in a hollow tree-trunk on the property, then introduce them surreptitiously.

All hell broke loose the day his wife discovered his hot stash and made it hotter still by setting fire to the lot.

I doubt Fergus ever brought any knickknacks home after that.

# Part Two

## The peace to end all peace

# Chapter Sixteen

By January 1952, Little Claude had suffered through St Columbas' and onto St James's School for advanced suffering. Patrice was starting her final year of torment at the local Catholic school. Young Russell still had a deal of training ahead before reaching his grandfather's goal to be the best five-eighth in Queensland. He was, after all, just starting grade two at the school of his elder sister - yet old enough to be thrilled by his grandfather's challenge.

From conversations with mother, I gather Russell could be a thoroughly endearing fellow. She told of a day he tricycled outside the confines of The Grand House. That this was forbidden had been impressed on him from a tender age. When she spied him joyfully riding the wild footpath, she grabbed the strap and headed downstairs intent on frightening the life out of him. As soon as he caught sight of his mother heading intently towards him with a scowl on her face and the nasty-looking deterrent in hand, he stopped in his tracks. For a brief moment he was completely still.

Then, as if totally oblivious to the scale of his impending correction, he pedalled towards her with a cherubic grin stretched across his face.

'Are we going to the flicks tonight, Mum?' he yelled with expectant glee.

This so instantly disarmed Ella, the strap dropped to her side and they both went upstairs to get ready for the Crystal Palace.

Russell used to have difficulty containing his exuberance for annual events, be they as grand as Christmas or as simple as Pancake Tuesday - when he knew mum would prepare a batch of freshly baked treats after school.

He had been late to class on this Pancake Day because he cut his foot, in the backyard. Ella had already replaced the bandage at least three times before he was finally ready to leave. She still vividly remembers telling him *this was the last time she intended strapping up his foot.*

On leaving, he begged mum to let him take the tram back home that afternoon, instead of the bus with his sister. The tram was quicker and he was as keen as mustard to be home. Ella finally acquiesced, after he convinced her he had paid attention to his road-safety instructions.

I was just over two, in February '52, hence I lack the memory of this tragedy. A car struck Russell as he disembarked from a tram, at virtually the same spot the houseguest once bowed before his nemesis.

As this tragedy was unfolding, Little Claude was riding home from St James's on a tram from the other direction, the Valley. He alighted and saw his brother lying motionless in the middle of Federation Street. He raced down the hill to report to his mother.

Almost simultaneously, Mickey's O'Rourke's daughter, Grace had been alerted to a serious incident involving one of Ella's boys, who she mistakenly believed to be Little Claude. She, too, rushed in the direction of her old friend's home, only to meet a panic-stricken Ella running towards the scene with Little Claude at her side.

Grace travelled in the ambulance with Ella to the general hospital, both knowing in their hearts that Russell was already dead. Ella kept looking at that bandaged little foot, shrinking at the thought of her prophetic words: *this is the last time I'm going to strap up your foot!*

Mrs. Grey looked after me on the day Russell was buried at Lutwyche Cemetery, after only six short years on this earth. Sometime after the funeral Ella searched for his last photo. It was a shot of him in school uniform, taken a few weeks earlier. She had that photo enlarged and framed, then placed on the dining-room wall with the others.

Russell's fate had a devastating effect on those of The Grand House old enough to comprehend (i.e., not me). The Old Man, who already exhibited moderate alcoholic tendencies, lost all moderation.

He was working for Patrick's Stevedoring on that grim day. By the time a phone message concerning his son's death filtered through, he had just finished afternoon tea-break and was back at work. I cringe to imagine the stings of alarm jabbing through his system, as he grabbed his Gladstone bag and scurried for the wharf gates. Here he was stopped and his premature departure questioned by a Patrick's employee.

Forcing back the agony, he related his heart-rending life crisis.

He was robotically informed that, because he hadn't completed his shift he was obliged to return his tea-money *before* he departed. Of course the Old Man had already spent the money on its intended purpose. I don't know exactly what blew up out of that. But for the rest of his life the Old Man harboured a profound and intense loathing of Patrick's Stevedoring.

They docked him the evening's wage, plus the tea-money.

Later that night, a couple of workmates called at The Grand House with a bottle of rum. That was the start of a bender that lasted for more than a week. It culminated in his being suspended for six months from the wharf, after reporting drunk for duty. He eventually sobered up and found a temporary job with the Nestlé factory in the Valley.

I vaguely remember the Nestlé period, for the way *His* wardrobe magically transformed into a cornucopia of chocolate.

After six months, he returned to the wharf. It seemed nothing would now curtail his excessive drinking. His workmates, including Fergus, were flat out trying to cover for him.

Financial mayhem arising from Russell's funeral expenses further compounded his distress. The Old Man had automatically taken out insurance for each of his children at birth. The policy paid out when the beneficiary reached twenty-one.

I suppose this might have guaranteed our financial security when we came of age. However, when Russell died, the Old Man was under the misguided impression that the proceeds of Russell's insurance would offset his funeral expenses. When he was informed he couldn't collect on the policy - because Russell fell several months short of their specified minimum of seven years - his bitterness towards insurance companies was only surpassed by his hatred for Patrick's Stevedoring. He promptly cancelled all our policies.

As the Old Man continued to drown his self-pity and anger, Ella had little choice but to suppress her emotions for the sake of her surviving children. Cecelia moved back to The Grand House with the exemplary intention of supporting her sister. However, she must have considered, if *the road to hell is paved with good intentions*, at least it had an internal toilet. She beat a hasty retreat to Mrs. Wren's.

I observed as I matured that adult siblings like Ella and Cecelia had difficulties cohabiting.

For her part, Patrice steadfastly refused to re-enter the school gates after Russell's demise. A sympathetic neighbour, with a young daughter my age stepped in with a solution. She was a hairdresser and got wind of an apprenticeship suitable for Patrice. However, she would need to lie about her age when applying.

Soon after, Patrice was taken on as an apprentice hairdresser with a popular salon in Adelaide Street. She started work at the tender age of thirteen. She was motivated by emotional devastation following grievous circumstances.

50

# Chapter Seventeen

Nothing would ever be quite the same at The Grand House.

Ella felt Claude harboured ill will toward her, for letting the boy cross the road unescorted. Patrice and Little Claude's childhood insouciance had gone. The Old Man had by now gained considerable momentum down the slippery slope to alcoholic ruin.

Ella felt powerless to impede any of these deleterious impulses.

She feared her life was tending to parallel her mother, Rebecca's. Neither husband allowed money shortages to stand in the way of drowning in a bottle. As a result, both wives engaged in a frenzied competition with the publicans each payday, to see who would get first go at lightening the wallet. The Old Man's preferred haunts were the Empire, the Prince Consort and the Royal George.

These are still landmarks of the Valley.

Mum related a poignant tale: one day she opened her purse to the heart-crushing realisation that she couldn't put food on the table that evening. Despondently, she placed baby in the pusher and, with Little Claude by her side, trekked up Bowen Bridge Road along Gregory Terrace, down past Roma Street rail-yards to reach Cecelia's workplace. She was hopeful of borrowing a few bob from her sister.

When it became apparent that Cecelia was, for whatever reason, bob free Ella had no option but to continue her thankless marathon. This time, she trudged towards the Valley with the forlorn hope of finding her husband in one of his regulars. Exhausted and dispirited, she peered through all the pub windows until she finally spotted him in the Empire.

This was before women were allowed in public bars, so she resorted to sending in Little Claude to draw out his father. She managed to extract barely enough for a pound of sausages and a tram ticket home.

The Old Man succeeded in holding down his job on the wharf, albeit with increasingly protracted intervals on worker's comp or sick-leave. His absenteeism was mostly attributable to alcohol. During these erratic times, he was fortunate to have loyal friends and workmates including his brother-in-law, who covered for him wherever possible.

I often wonder if Fergus's two boys share so improbable a strain of memory, having also being raised by waterside workers in the fifties and early sixties.

The quirky nicknames they bestowed each other still tickle the odd rib. 'London Fog' was the bloke who never lifted (anything). The bloke called 'Hydraulic,' on the other hand, could lift anything. (I'm not sure whether the epithet referred to his willingness to lift heavy objects or his aptitude for pilfering.) Another that springs to mind is 'Postage Stamp,' who just sat in the corner for his entire shift. Even the shifts themselves were dubbed - such as 'Midnighter' or 'Freezing.'

If The Old Man was on Freezing, he needed to pad out in his warmest. The balaclava, too, because he could be unloading frozen produce from the bowels of the ship for the duration. All waterside workers carried Gladstone bags, in which they stashed a sinister-looking hook. If The Old Man was on a Midnighter the smell of toast would waft through The Grand House in the deep of night. Mum was preparing a late supper before he headed to work on the last tram.

My most vivid memories were of early mornings, when the wireless would be tuned in for the duty roster. The sounds of 'Anchors Away, My Boys' anticipated the recitation of personnel numbers: waterside workers who had work that day. We all listened intently for The Old Man's number, while Ella quietly prayed he would be in shape to arrive on time.

One particular annual festival ensured the wharves' desertion. Melbourne Cup Day was also Wharfie's Picnic Day. In the fifties, union membership numbered in the thousands, meaning the outdoors *picnic* amounted to a great seething throng. It was a true family affair and no expense was spared on thrilling the kids. The event was traditionally at Shorncliffe Beach (apart from one year when they changed it to the RNA showgrounds).

Ella, Claude and entourage (including me) would be done up like sore toes in our Sunday best, waiting at the tram stop at the back of The Grand House. We would jostle for a spot among the crowd heading for work, on the first tram to the city. It was standing room only in the stifling November heat for the short ride to Brunswick Street Station. Here, we would hop on the old, wooden shake-rattle-and-roll steam-train waiting to jiggle us all the way to Shorncliffe.

One year, almost every woman, girl and even the odd man-child waiting on the platform were decked out in a variety of individually tailored outfits, all made from the same fabric. (The stuff had obviously fallen off the back of a crate in the past week or two.)

The train ride was endlessly thrilling for us: we of The Grand House rarely experienced trains. We were familiar with trams as the Chermside, Stafford and Grange tram-services passed the back of the house. But a train was like the real thing (the tram was Clayton's).

On arrival at Shorncliffe, we would be squeaking with delight, falling over ourselves to disembark. We then galloped up the hill, straining for a first glimpse of the ocean. Once the sea was in view, the chatter and giggling would fall silent in an intense and desperate scramble down steep slopes overgrown with lantana to the beach below.

Scattered over the beachfront were merry-go-rounds and stalls offering fairy-floss, toffee-apples, boiled lollies, ice blocks and ice-creams. The stalls heating giant pans in the giant heat, created a brash clash like brassy cymbals, the hot air burnt still from the aroma of sugar caramelising.

Every child was issued with a handful of vouchers for assorted foodstuffs and rides. A dependable eye-opener was a performance of the now politically incorrect Punch & Judy show.

Old Punch goes back quite a few centuries and he's the archetypal anarchist. Punch, the less than personable puppet starts out by shaking and strangling the living daylights out of his good wife, Judy. If she carried a baby then he first entices her to give it to him. After constant refusals, he grabs the baby but loses it. He attempts to substitute a crocodile in a blanket and finally resorts to hammering her over the head with it. He then tears the truncheon away from the arresting cop and proceeds to beat the crap out of him. He tops off the performance by hanging the hangman. It all seems quite logical when you're a child (bit like a Bruce Willis movie these days). The enjoyment of the day was heightened no end by the fact that we would otherwise have been at school.

There was ample time for a stroll along the pier and a dip in the ocean, if one happened to be inclined. I was never overly fond of water, since Little Claude threw me in at the Spring Hill baths. Apparently, that was his preferred technique for swim coaching. I was as about as likely to learn swimming that way as I would to read, by being hit over the head with a book. Even if I could swim, injuries from jellyfish and sea-lice were a chilling disincentive. (I'm just not the sort of girl who likes sitting around in cold puddles.)

Once the Melbourne Cup had blared out over loudspeakers, we knew it as the cue to begin trekking back over the hill to the waiting train.

# Chapter Eighteen

For some reason, Little Claude desperately hated the idea of completing primary school at St James's. He stressed to his mother the desirability of her transferring him to the nearby Windsor State School for the start of year eight. He painted several options to this transfer, all of them quite spine-chilling scenarios. There's no doubt Little Claude was as bright as a button. He had already been proclaimed the dux of the school (which came with the scholarly and culturally relevant prize of a *Biggles* book).

What the catalyst was for changing schools at this late stage, I can only guess, perhaps with some plausibility, to have been the stern methods of the Christian Brothers. Mind you, if the Brothers *were* strict with Little Claude it wouldn't have been without justification. For as much as he seemed a bit soft or a mummy's boy in The Grand House, his behaviour beyond it was a complete paradox. I don't recall him ever backing away from a fight. To this day, he adds a quixotic flavour to the family hotchpotch with larger-than-life exploits and adventures.

Ella was agreeable to the change of schools. There again, I seriously doubt if any request from her firstborn boy would have seemed too troublesome. With Little Claude's departure from St James's it would be a long time before any member of The Grand House went near a Catholic school or church again.

From that juncture religion played little or no part in any of our lives.

I have often wondered whether this spiritual recalcitrance in the family (who would, till then, have scored divinely on a *Catholicometer*) had anything to do with disillusionment on our mother's part. If their god metes out fate: he had tragically killed one too many nearest and dearest to warrant her respect. Anyway, for whatever reason, Royce and I cultivated identities in our formative years - the decade of the 'fifties - as *the little heathens* of the neighbourhood.

Since Royce was the elder, he was the first to start school. Suggesting Royce *started* school sounds incongruous. Mum dragged him kicking and screaming on the first day (quite an earful all the way from The Grand House). By the time she arrived home, her sense of *mission accomplished* was rudely displaced on finding him there, waiting. This became a routine. Those days when he did stay, he whiled away in the sandpit just below the grade-one classroom window at Little School (as we knew it). Hardly surprising, then, Royce needed to repeat his first year. This was encouraging: it granted me an opportunity to catch up, starting just one grade behind.

I 'commenced' school in 1955 the year Little Claude was finishing. Only Royce's aversion to school surpassed mine. We spent our entire primary years contriving every imaginable mad scheme to avoid attendance. You could count on one finger the number of weeks we were present on all five days, and on two fingers the symbol we counted on. If either of us were legitimately sick the other would stay out in sympathy.

The day I broke my leg in a fall, while running under school buildings, I was dispatched to the children's hospital in an ambulance. I spent several weeks in hospital before being sent home to convalesce. Royce was so miffed by my good fortune: I'm sure he was contriving all sorts of theatrical ways to break a leg.

Like my mother before me, I hated everything about school. The artlessly functional structure, jaded by the rank stench of phenol was so determinably repugnant. I despised the deafening clanging from a brass bell summonsing me to the black, asphalt parade ground, devoid of greenery. The tedious *rrrrat tat tat . . . rrat tat tat* of the school drummer clattered with an irritating staccato, like a bored child drumming fingernails. I was drummed up the stairs to abide the torment of 'class' with the other prisoners. Funny, if there's one thing they just *never* had, it was class. There was a permanent stink of egg-sandwiches. (This impoverished snack still makes me wince.)

The dank and dingy under buildings (*running strictly forbidden*) were set in a sea of desolate grey concrete within a perimeter of wooden forms. I remember being made to sit on those hard places and force-fed free milk. The free milk scheme, supposedly designed to provide minimum daily calcium, achieved exactly the opposite for me.

Those loathsome little bottles arrived well before the most dedicated nerd. They then spent the interlude to *little lunch* soaking up warm morning rays. By the time the rapidly souring liquid passed my lips (under the menace of the prison officer on playground duty) it was likely to do anything but enhance health. The aftermath was the dribbled, spilt and otherwise remaining milk built up a memorable stench. At the first possible opportunity, I would bolt to the nearest

56

drinking trough and wash down what I couldn't spit out. To this day, I need milk to be chilled beyond any chance of that smell recurring.

Nevertheless, if you took school out of the equation, which Royce and I mostly did, the truant episodes meant life in the fifties was vibrant with escapist thrills and spills.

The only noxious moment during an off-school day was the weekly visit by the debt collector from a department store in the Valley. In those days, this store used to employ salesmen door-to-door to peddle all manner of things, including their own in-house currency. The same salesman collected payments on outstanding debts. I shudder to think what the terms of credit were. I doubt whether the poor wretches they targeted, including Ella, ever thought about the rate of interest. Purchasing on the never-never was the only way they could see themselves acquiring substantial items. It never ever seemed to cross their minds the extent to which they were digging themselves deeper into debt. I expect Ella lived with the vain hope of that elusive win on the Casket or on the horses, which would bail her out of destitution.

Anyway, the debt collector came on Mondays. Since that was the first day of the school week, there was a reasonable chance either Royce or I, or both, would have been too sick to put in an appearance at school. It was an erratic type of malaise that usually reached fever pitch between 7 and 9, then subsided miraculously around midmorning (a great relief to all).

When Ella spied the familiar car, she would draw the curtains in the front room and wait for a knock on the door. That was our cue to scamper out with the story about our mother having been called away somewhere on urgent business. We weren't sure where she went nor when she was coming back.

I have no doubt, whatsoever, he was 100% sure this pathetic excuse was a barefaced lie. Being such hopeless liars, we heaved audible sighs of relief as he walked back downstairs. The rocky part of the day having been overcome, it was back to the comic books.

Incidentally, during those years I recall several instances when large household items appeared then vanished a short time later. They were probably repossessed.

# Chapter Nineteen

The best of my fading memories of the fifties comes from school holidays with Royce. Because Christmas coincided with the largest chunk of time off, it was far and away our favourite part of the year. Mum loved Christmas, despite the fact that it started with top-to-bottom house cleaning, several weeks out from the big day.

She would produce the Silvo from somewhere at the back of the crowded kitchen cupboard and polish the trophies, lined up on the silky-oak sideboard in the dining room. These included Pa's boxing and football cups as well as The Old Man's yachting prizes.

Then the curtains came down for their annual clean. Whilst they were out on clothes' lines propped aloft on wooden staves, the lino would be polished. A brilliant shine was achieved by applying polish on hands and knees with an old rag dipped into a round tin of wax. This would then be removed using an electric polisher, which I presume she borrowed. I say this because I only ever laid eyes on it in the lead up to Christmas.

This remarkable, though stridently screaming piece of equipment consisted of two rotating lamb's-wool pads affixed to a motor unit. It was encased in a Bakelite shell whose bulbous no-corners appearance was, as with the cars of the time, a contemporary stylistic trend. It had an oblong light at the front to facilitate admiration of work in progress. As the lamb's-wool rotated at 78 r.p.m. across the surface, the dull lino would take a new interest in life (everyone loved *shiny* in those days).

A potentially lethal dance, after the mats and door slips had been put back was frequently staged by impromptu performance. It usually started with a glissade, which was then followed by *pas de Basque,* RF LF LF RF and subsequent splits. This performance was likely to be set to the music of *The Death Throes of the Wailing Banshee* (composer unknown).

Christmas Eve and final touches were fresh flowers and, of course, the Christmas tree. For the former, Royce or I would need to pay a visit to the flower lady. Mrs. Walker down the street was dainty and withered, in vivid contrast to her entire front yard, which flushed with an artist's palette of seasonal blooms. For a shilling, she would cheerfully cut a huge armful and wrap the stems in newspaper for the trip home.

The boys, ably led by Little Claude would be in charge of fetching the tree from another close neighbour, whose claim to fame was having the world's biggest camphor-laurel in his backyard. Axe in hand, Little Claude would disappear into the midst of its giant canopy in search of exactly the right bough. It had to be large enough to make a spectacular display, yet small enough to be dragged up the back steps and through the doorway.

Little Claude always came through on the day. Before long, we would be battling to make it stand *sort of* upright inside an old tin drum filled with rocks, stones and broken bricks. Then, like a theatre prop, it had to be secured to the wall at the back with some string and drawing-pins (kept in the yachting trophy cups).

Once in place, it was invariably Patrice who decorated the tree from a gigantic box of ornaments and tinsel kept on *Hers* wardrobe. She was always given this job and that used to really needle me: I always seemed to be fuming at my sister's store of privileges.

There's nothing like those beautifully ornamented trees you see on Christmas cards. And ours was certainly nothing like them. Nevertheless, the collective creation allowed for a deeply satisfying, albeit appallingly shambolic outcome.

Our dire shortage of money at The Grand House was never further from my thoughts than on waking each Christmas morning to an abundance of presents (mostly handmade by Dad) under the tree.

Christmas lunch was a major production, with a cast of what seemed like thousands. Actually, it was more like twenty, if Uncle Fergus's family joined us. We all sat around the giant wooden table (after a phalanx of slaves had transported it to the dining room). Even it often had to be supplemented with a temporary extension. You could hardly notice the old Singer, with a piece of ply and a few gorgeous throws.

There were always enough lollies encircled by assorted bowls of nuts and chocolates to ruin the appetite. Despite strict instructions, I barely ever resisted. Inevitably, when roast dinner was served like a threat at precisely midday, eating it felt like stretching the stomach's sense of seasonal duty beyond the ridiculous.

Oblivious to stifling temperatures, Christmas dinner was always larded with the same traditional northern-hemisphere winter fare. Because you need cholesterol for galvanising the body to combat freezing winds, a first course of diverse stuffed roast meats and poultry, accompanied with baked vegetables, all dripping with oil and topped with viscous gravy would be just the thing for Christmas dinner *in England.*

Inappropriate mains having been dispensed with in record time, the sweat liberally pouring off our faces, a second course of hot plum-pudding smothered in glutinous globs of custard was served. Mum baked threepences into our Christmas pudding. To our disgust and annoyance Paddy consumed most of them without batting an eyelid.

It must have been a marathon chore preparing and serving a meal on such a grand scale, with temperatures in the high nineties (the fifties were still Fahrenheit). All that, on top of weeks spent readying the house for guests. Hardly surprising, then, mum was motivated by getting everything over and done with as speedily as possible so she could finally relax. This anticipated moment of repose produced such a delirious whirlwind of activity: the serving and consuming of two courses must have taken less than fifteen minutes.

The euphoria of Christmas would abruptly turn to bathos on our first visit back to the Valley. The store windows were now drably functional with Back to School promotions. It felt as though my best friend had suddenly turned nasty. Christmas is something to celebrate, simply because of the pleasure principle; it's art for art's sake.

When I was a child, the Valley was Christmas Central. It out-splendoured the nearby shopping centre in town. Santa arrived in the Valley, not the town, with a big procession in late November. After his flourishing appearance, he played piano on the roof over the entrance to McWhirters. The windows of that store were devoted to magical and fairytale themes. Then other retailers large and small followed, hanging lights and decorations in abundance throughout their shops, sometimes spilling into the streets outside.

Now, overnight, it was all gone.

An abandoned feeling descended on Royce and me, as we recoiled at being the defenceless victims of regimentation. Holiday thoughts would be hourly tormented by what lay ahead at the end of January: we would be forced to return to that bleak redbrick institution.

# Chapter Twenty

From the first day of the new school year, Royce and I hung out like a couple of addicts for the next hit of holiday, which was Easter. In the fifties Easter was nothing more than a Friday and a Monday tagged onto the regular weekend. Our holidays otherwise consisted of a fortnight's break in both May and August. Mind you, there were no complaints from either of us; it was *any old port in the storm* as far as holidays went.

The Easter bunny came to The Grand House on Friday morning which is what, I consequently surmised, made it Good. For many years I was unaware most children weren't given their eggs till Sunday. For Royce and I, the religious significance of the period was a bit abstract. We were too busy making the most of this brief respite from school.

Once Easter was behind us, we counted down the remaining school days until the two-week extended May vacation. This coincided with the Labour Day procession. The May Day march back then was a major happening compared to its piddling apology nowadays. There were literally dozens of floats interspersed with marching girls and pipe-bands, all afoot in solidarity with hundreds of unionists. As I remember, it commenced at Centenary Park then proceeded through the Valley to conclude at the Ekka grounds.

The Old Man never missed being in the starting line up, under the banner of the Waterside Worker's Federation. For all his show of solidarity, however, he could never quite seem to make it past The Shamrock to the finish line. Mum would be in the enormous crowd with us kids, around the front of McDonald's Cake Shop in Brunswick Street. We had to arrive really early to secure a view.

A front vantage-point guaranteed you would have the daylights scared out of you by the devils. These were members of the Printers' Union who dressed in red costumes, complete with horns and tails and carrying menacing pitchforks.

Once the huge procession had passed, mum would duck into McDonald's for a loaf of freshly baked bread. Then we would make tracks home to devour it while still warm. Little in life tastes better than freshly baked bread, cut into thick, uneven slices, spread liberally with butter and Vegemite.

Once the May holidays had passed, Royce and I would trudge our way back to school through the bleak winter, bracing for the onset of the westerly winds.

The westerlies traditionally ushered in the Ekka. From The Grand House it was just a stroll to the showgrounds. In preceding weeks, we would have noted the sideshow rides taking shape as we passed in the tram, on trips to the Valley.

This event cued some serious fund raising for People's Day. There were a number of reliable ways to accumulate capital in those days. Royce was always guaranteed a shilling a week for polishing Paddy's shoes. This was in readiness for his Saturday outing to the Shamrock, now his local. Another penny or two could be made selling old newspapers back to the corner store and old bottles to a dealer in Swan Terrace. A wooden cart, which was probably made by the Old Man, proved ideal for both tasks.

Golden earning opportunities for Royce and me came when this well-spoken chap took up the rear flat in the neighbouring duplex. He worked as a radio announcer. Elocution was his specialty: his consonants were spoken as exactly as a pin dropped onto a marble floor.

Every Saturday morning he would employ us to fetch his weekly shopping. List and money in hand, we painstakingly ensured every item exactly matched what was written before returning it to his back steps. The task completed to his satisfaction, he would first thank us profusely then hand over all the silver coins in the change. This would often include a florin or two.

'Buy yourselves a battleship!' he then said, in his proper voice.

(I always imagined this to be some oblique reference to the old tug in our backyard.)

If we were still strapped for cash by the time People's Day morning came around we could, more often than not, entice the Old Man to supplement our kitty. Where possible, we reached our target of fifteen bob in hand, before excitedly heading for the showgrounds with mum and dad.

That was the sum necessary to buy five sample bags.

Royce and I were a little too immature to be purchasing fear on the rides. The horror on the faces of the older kids as they hopped off the Chair-O-Plane, or emerged from the Ghost Train made us thankful for our youthful naïveté. There was a mandatory stop, along Sideshow Alley for a bottle of milk dyed pink and a Dagwood dog on a stick. Once we reached the Industrial Pavilion, some serious decisions had to be made. This was where we stood to be relieved of the rest of our money. So we concentrated intently and earnestly debated the merits of each separate case: was it to be the Nestlé, Cadbury, Lifesaver, Hoadley-Fry, MacRobertson or Liquorice Bag? If a peek inside the bag before purchase revealed a Phantom comic, then it was guaranteed selection. The Old Man loved Phantom and Mandrake, so we could score points by passing them on. Equally, a Queen bag always scored with mum although there was nothing to rot teeth inside to appeal to us.

Having squandered all our hard-earned cash we paraded proudly home loaded to the hilt with bags. On arrival, we would promptly dump the contents over our beds to take stock and insist on preferences. Bartering could become quite heated when tastes coincided, even to the point of needing a referee.

It took few days to consume the stockpile of sweets and even less to smash, tread on, break or lose the plastic frippery bits and pieces that came with them.

Then life went back to normal. Monday morning before breakfast, flu sets in. Matches worked well held some distance under the thermometer, before mum returned to check.

# Chapter Twenty One

For Royce and I in our pre-teens, Saturday was the paramount event of the week (notwithstanding school or public holidays). It was the only day of the week our imaginations touched down for a terrestrial view.

The background soundtrack to Saturday was the tinny crescendos of races on the wireless; mum listened intently to hear if her previous night's selection would be the miracle of her earthly salvation. Commenting as one ill-disposed to punting, the implausible optimism of those who have this disposition never ceases to amaze. It's difficult enough selecting a *single* winner. Is it then some desperate, screaming optimism or a profound dedication to irrational behaviour that causes addicted punters to take out Trifectas?

On days mum couldn't get a Trifecta placed with the SP bookie (whose tradesman disguise I had now *Sherlocked*), Royce and me found ourselves obligingly trotting up to Mrs. Wren's in Bowen Hills on Saturday mornings. On arrival, we would hand Cecelia a note containing the names of 'likely' horses, so she could take out the Trifecta for mum. She would place the bet that afternoon while down at the track.

Some Saturdays, mum would actually take the tram down to Doomben or Eagle Farm. On a number of occasions, she was unavoidably delayed because she had to walk home, having blown the tram fare on a sure thing. Once home, she would dutifully light the wood-stove to serve tea before we headed up to the Crystal Palace.

Movies were exceptional value. Somehow, I doubt people could sit still for long enough these days. For a paltry admission fee we could expect two feature films, a cartoon and the Movietone News.

We kept chooks and I was terrified of one particular rooster, called Banty. Mum used this fear to her advantage, to keep me from misbehaving at the movies one Saturday night. One of Banty's feathers on the floor in front of my seat and even the horrors of *The Thing*, which crawled down theatre aisles during the movie to disappear into people's spines paled to insignificance.

The Crystal Palace was the meet-market for the neighbourhood during the fifties. Not only did almost every kid in the district turn up for the Saturday matinée, it was also the venue for *Norman Llewellyn's Rumpus Room* broadcast live over the radio.

Part of the program's ritual was a treasure hunt into the neighbourhood, in which Little Claude once triumphed. There were also competitions conducted from a stage. Royce was the star of one particular performance. They offered a prize for the person who could recite in its entirety the radio advertisement for Redskin's Peanuts. Royce strode up to the microphone and burst out in the most baleful monotone:

> *Says big chief Redskin in a Pow Pow.*
> *Salted Redskin Peanuts heap big Wow Wow.*
> *Now instead of going scalpin'*
> *we stay and eat 'em second helpin'.*
> *Redskin Peanuts heap good munchin'.*
> *Salty Tangy when you crunch'em.*
> *Go buy Redskin Peanuts now.*
> *You'll like them Kernel Redskin. How!*

He finished with a fierce war cry made by yelling and simultaneously moving his stiff hand on and off his mouth, just like he had seen Red Indians do in our weekly intake of Westerns. The war cry was so piercing after his indifferent mumbling of the text, they all woke with a start. For that rousing demonstration of subliminal thought-control and the brainwashing potential of vapid advertising he won thirty bob (and the enduring respect of every kid in the live audience or listening at home, on 4BH).

My memories include a promotion sponsored by Coca-Cola. A wireless announcement would specify where their truck was to be. The first to reach it got a freebie. One April Fool's day sticks in my throat. Little Claude raved wildly at me that the truck was coming to a corner several blocks away. The lure of a bottle of Coke was more than I could resist, so I ran my skinny little legs off. (The household budget back then barely extended to a bottle of GI lime cordial. Thirsts were generally slaked at the downstairs tap, from cupped hands.) Of course, I found on arriving at the street corner wheezing, gasping and buckled over with stitches, it was all a big bad Coke joke. Little Claude was cacking himself laughing when I got back.

Sunday was always a depressing day for Royce and me. Just the mere thought of what lay ahead on Monday turned it into a damper.

Sundays were synonymous with baked mutton at midday, followed occasionally by a walk with mum and the Old Man bringing up the rear to the nearby museum. After a circuit of the majestic old building ('Stop running! Don't shout! No shoving in front of the displays!') we would return to a cold tea of leftover meat with salad.

Nothing ever changed at the dusty old museum, guarded outside by enormous dinosaurs and a German tank. A plane suspended from the ceiling, hundreds of dead butterflies and assorted dry creatures under glass cabinets wasn't exactly a ticket to Thrillsville for me.

I was more intrigued with the Renaissance castle-like museum building itself. I would muse starry-eyed at the wonder of what life could be like, given everywhere you looked was a magnificent flourish of artistry, sculpture and style. Mum tells me that Dame Nellie Melba performed in the art gallery on two occasions. The art gallery was a latter addition to the museum. We never went quite *that* culturally astray on our Sunday excursions.

Nowadays the sorry old structure, in dire need of repair, is home to the Queensland Youth Symphony Orchestra. Their Sunday twilight concerts are well worth taking in.

Another grand old edifice, typifying the style of a bygone era although not nearly as magnificent as the museum, was the Oddfellows Hall at the back of The Grand House. This unadorned wooden structure was entered via a ramp from the footpath: the land fell away sharply from high front to back drop. It was perched on tree-length wooden stumps at the rear, underneath which toilets were accessed by a flight of wooden stairs. The plain wooden front door was normally bolted, except for wedding receptions or on election days.

Like his father before him, the Old Man was a dyed-in-the-wool Labor supporter. He could always be called on to do his bit for the party when elections came around. When the polls opened on Saturday morning, he would be in place outside the hall enthusiastically offering voting guides to all and sundry. We kids loved to hang around and collect the disused cards. In a few short hours, we could amass so many hundreds of them.

Inevitably, by Saturday afternoon there was no sign of the Old Man at Oddfellows Hall. He would be dissolving all that political rage, and the rage of his personal slights, holding up the bar of the Empire in the Valley.

Alcohol is the opiate of the masses.

# Chapter Twenty Two

During the fifties, the ethnic background of those living around The Grand House gradually diversified from its English and Irish beginnings. Italians had already begun to spice up the neighbourhood. They typically constructed imposing brick residences abundantly girded with ornate cement balustrades. Their front yards often featured concrete birdbaths topped by scantily clad cherubs frolicking with musical instruments. Every square inch of real estate was swathed in concrete. It's a great Latin tradition. As Julius Caesar once avowed when he brought civilisation to the barbarians of Briton: *I come, I see, I concrete.* Back then, of course, more human bones made up the mix than would be likely today.

Caesar's splendid abode was diagonally opposite the fibro flats. Smells from their kitchen around seven o'clock used to have me sniffing the air with a whole new concept of delicious welling up in my mind. I was yet to discover Mediterranean food.

In 1956, a migrant couple with three teenage children bought two doors up the hill from The Grand House. They were White Russians (i.e., aristocrats or capitalists, including many Jews, ousted by the Reds or Bolsheviks). As a green seven-year old with a colourful imagination, the concept of a 'White' Russian fascinated me. I pondered what colours these mysterious people might be capable of manifesting.

Two of the daughters had been born in a concentration camp in the last war. The father had a highly qualified profession back in the old country but his degrees (from one of the most ancient and respected universities in Europe) and publications weren't acknowledged in Australia. Not surprisingly, this was a bitter disappointment to him and a financial disaster for his family.

That alone would have been excuse enough for his tendency to marinate in vodka with his ethnic peers. This, I'm led to believe all took place in his home, like some fate-strapped madcap out of a Dostoyevsky novel. His wife spoke with an accent so pronounced, communication was a labour of love. From her demeanour and expressions, she gave all the appearances of being a long-suffering, kind and affable woman.

You have to admire their courage in coming to a new country where the language and customs are strange (and xenophobia hides in dark corners). She and her family had been hounded, robbed, persecuted and threatened for the first half of the twentieth century. I vaguely recall one of the daughters staging her wedding reception in the Oddfellows Hall, not long after the family moved in. The chap she married had an English surname. Their children reveal little trace of their poor mother's ethnic origins. Hopefully, their worst nightmares will be nothing compared to the suffering she endured.

The house up the hill from the Russians belonged to a family with the infamous Irish name of Maroney. That name will be indelibly printed on my mind: one of their sons was the bane of my inner-child. Neville Maroney was my age. It became his personal obsession to intimidate me whenever I stepped outside the yard, alone. He seemed to have a sixth sense as to when this would be. Without fail, Neville would bail me up against a wall or fence, and threaten to thrash me.

I can't actually recall if he ever did. The unprovoked hostility made me scurry back home crying my eyes out. My horizons had suddenly blackened: I was fenced in like a dog. The freedom to play, and share in the invigorating and creative impulses play inspires, had been swiftly and stealthily taken from me. The streets lost their tribal feel and became alienating alleys. Mum had no end of trouble convincing me to go to the shop.

I could have patented some of the inventions I dreamt up to get out of it. There was a particular time that sits like a splinter encrusted with defensive thoughts. I was cajoled into a solo safari up the urban jungle for a packet of Billy Tea. Gingerly, I left the safety of the front yard and nervously strutted to the corner. At that point I stood and stared awhile breathing heavily, the pulse throbbing in my veins and the electric quiver of hunted-animal fear in my skin.

I still had to negotiate a long footpath leading uphill, before reaching the safety of the busy main-road. I knew my cowardly assailant would never dare display his bullying so visibly. I edged my way up past the neighbouring duplex. This was where Neville tended to lurk, on the last leg of my return trips. A small section of the footpath was beyond window-view and ideal for an ambush.

The thought of what might be up ahead, should I dare to continue with this folly was too hideous. I owed it to my parents not to become another nail in the family coffin. I turned round and dashed home to tell mum the shop was out of tea.

I never set foot inside Maroney's house. At first glance, theirs was a typical worker's cottage on sixteen perches not unlike most others in the street. It was only on zoom lens that the fastidiously whistle-clean look of the place became apparent. The red paint from the concrete path, up the wooden front-stairs was so liquid-smooth not the lightest of creatures could have laid footprint there.

I have it on good authority from Uncle Fergus, who made grocery deliveries to the house (via the backdoor, of course) that the inside was indeed an immaculate conception. The lady of the house was a pinpoint perfectionist. No-one, including her own family, its dog or a neighbour's stifled sneeze was allowed inside before removing its shoes.

Far from being a chip off the old block, her kids suffered RDD: repressed disorder disorder. This meant they used to wreak havoc everywhere else, including The Grand House like an explosive gala opening of Pandora's Box. The fact that the man of the house was a tipsy old soak was perfectly normal as far as I was concerned; however, their children were a paranormally intriguing bunch. I can no longer recall their number or names. There was a boy around Little Claude's age and a girl not much older than Patrice.

Years later, I learnt Maroney's daughter used to intimidate Patrice, as Neville tormented me. Of course Little Claude suffered no similar indignity with his Maroney peer. (Or, he would only ever try it once.) Quite the reverse, Little Claude and Paul Maroney rode the tram together to and from St James's. What's more, Paul happened to be with him on that ghastly afternoon when Russell was killed.

In hindsight, the boy who was my nemesis transformed into a highly intriguing character. His family's backyard had disused stables like ours. Neville had cleaned them to perfection, for use as his cubby-house. An integral feature of these renovations was the heavily montaged walls, layered with posters collected from the Crystal Palace. He had obviously reached an understanding with the proprietor about his Parisian-café taste in wallpaper.

Neville's vintage collection of Bette Davis, Joan Crawford and Clark Gable posters would fetch a small fortune today. He also had another fascinating cultural pursuit. He enjoyed nothing more than putting on his mother's dresses and her high-heels in order to strut his stuff in glorious, pouting, hip-swirling action down the street!

I can't remember exactly when that family moved out. It couldn't have been soon enough for me. Their girl of Patrice's age married a fellow who used to beat her. If I'm not mistaken, she took her own life. I heard Paul did a stint at Her Majesty's expense. Neville became a successful interior decorator (during the day).

The next uphill from Maroney's housed a likeable larrikin called Errol-John. He and my brothers hung out together. Errol-John was *sort of* an only child to Mr & Mrs C. They, without doubt, would take the Golden Heart Award as the kindest people in the street. I should explain what I meant by his being a *sort of* only child.

Errol-John's father had lived up the road from The Grand House for ages. He remarried sometime after his first wife passed away. The second Mrs. C. was Errol-John's mother; he was their only child. Out of interest, it was the first Mrs. C who introduced Ella into society. (She took her to her first dance, at Broadway in the Valley.)

The second Mrs. C. - the only one I knew - already had some grown-up children by the time of her marriage to Mr. C.

The youngest from her first marriage moved in to occupy the front sleep-out when she remarried.

As a *sort of* only child, Errol-John didn't seem too deprived (at least compared to the privations we endured at The Grand House). Errol-John was so loyal a friend to my brothers: he never missed a wharfie picnic - despite Mr. C. never having been a wharfie in his life.

Because I was the infant of the family, Errol-John called me Bubba. If he and my brothers wanted to give me the slip, they would tell me mother was calling. By the time I found out it wasn't true, they would be gone. When Errol-John did deign to include me, it was usually at the expense of one of my dolls.

There was one large rag doll called Marilyn. The Old Man had won it in a raffle in the Valley. Errol-John would tie her onto the clothesline then belt her with a broom till she was raggedly out of sorts. At that point he would tell me Marilyn was drunk, so she had to be thrown into Paddy's room until she sobered up.

Later, if he was still at a loose end, he would retrieve her, tell me she wasn't sober yet then repeat the whole process. As you might expect, it wasn't long before poor Marilyn fell apart. My bride-doll fared no better under the reign of terror from Errol-John and cohorts. (Mum told me, because I so desperately wanted a bride-doll from Santa, she had rushed to the Valley on Christmas Eve and bought a bare one. She spent the remainder of the night making it into a bride, using scraps of material from around the place.) Before the dust had settled on the New Year celebrations, Errol-John and the boys gave her long, golden locks a trim. I was too young at the time to remember either of these dolly episodes. However, mum vouches for their poignancy.

Standing tall in my memory are so many kind deeds from Mr. & Mrs. C. over the years. Mr. C. always referred to Royce as Smiley: he reckoned Royce was a dead-ringer for the star character in the cinematic adventures of *The Adventures of a Boy Called Smiley*. That was a popular movie in the fifties starring Chips Rafferty, and a young lad named Colin Peterson if my memory serves me well.

People seemed to stay put for much longer in those days. Neighbours seem to come and go in such quick succession now.

Or perhaps it's just *my* neighbours!

Some examples of long tenure around The Grand House during the fifties were, of course Mr. and Mrs. C. Coming a close second would be the two spinster sisters in the next house but one, up the hill. These two were the nieces of the councillor-and-shopkeeper, who had a local park named after him. God only knows how long they had been living there by the fifties. In those days, the cottage opposite The Grand House was still occupied by offspring of the Masonic-Lodge personality of yore. A truce must have been declared in the intervening years. At least, I noted no particularly colourful language exchanges while growing up.

The next-door cottage remained rented by the O'Shea family for many years after Rebecca first helped them with a week's rent. In the intervening period all the sons had moved out, for one reason or another, leaving the daughter who was a couple of years older than my mother at home with her parents.

During the early forties one of the sons lived there with his wife, during which time they spawned a couple of boys. That coincided with when Royce was the baby of the house. Mum remembers that, because the two boy-tots used to refer to her as *Mummy Royce*. The spinster daughter and her parents finally purchased the house from their ailing landlord. Soon after the acquisition, the cottage underwent a radical transformation including the installation of an upstairs bathroom and toilet, along with a hot-water system.

Grace O'Rourke and her bachelor brothers continued to abide in the vicinity during the fifties. Grace remained single. Shamus O'Rourke never missed calling in to The Grand House around Christmas with a gift-box of biscuits or the like, for Ella. If feeling particularly zesty, he would turn a couple of cartwheels down the hallway as he left.

# Chapter Twenty Three

During the fifties Royce helped the Old Man do up the boat. This training held him in good stead years later when he constructed a smaller craft on his tod. I'm assuming renovations on the hefty old tug were completed around the middle of that decade because it disappeared. I believe it was sold.

Royce and Pa used to spend time together in the days when horses and betting were a common denominator. Royce loved animals in general and horses in particular. His dream lacked only the manhood and a set from Snowy River. Past remnants of horse habitation at The Grand House were a potent lure: the ruined stables still substituted for a back fence. The Lone Ranger could be found there on rainy days, bragging about who could ride the fastest out of town.

Using the backyard folly as leverage, he would regularly implore Pa to shrug off all this newfangled mechanical rubbish and go back to the horse, just like the good old days.

I don't know if Pa simply capitulated for a moment's peace and quiet or whether Royce had entirely misunderstood what had been agreed.

Royce spent a whole day excitedly repairing the old stables in readiness for a horse. Pa was supposedly bringing one home that night. Poor Royce was totally devastated when he arrived with a collie-cross puppy instead of a Clydesdale pony. Royce, being the gentle natured person he was (and still is) didn't take long to overcome his disappointment. He named the puppy, Horse.

To me, Horse will always be the pet associated with growing up. Owning a dog in those days was comparatively easygoing, chore-wise. Today the ever-vigilant dogcatchers lurk in readiness to slap a hefty on-the-spot fine should you so much as set foot outside the yard without four-legs leashed up.

In vivid contrast, Horse roamed the neighbourhood with the boys and their friends from daylight to dusk. Mum could relax in confidence: no-one would lay a hand on the kids as long as Horse was with them. Wherever they went Horse went too, including in and out of the creek.

Incidentally, the creek I remember bore little resemblance to its picturesque description from a couple of chapters ago. Industry was infiltrating and the creek was suffering its toxic aftermath. Although Horse loved nothing better than to begrime in the rank and foetid slime; he hated being washed. He could predict an ambush whenever the tin bucket and canvas hose appeared on his horizon. From there on out, he would deploy every devious, underhand tactic of canine cunning to get away. It always seemed a mystery why we bothered. Only seconds out from the cleaning fiasco – with us looking more washed than Horse – he would roll around in the dirt until he got that comfortable feeling of grit back into his fur.

As Royce and I grew into teenagers, poor Horse grew into a mangy flea-bitten version of his former sleek, trim, taut and terrific puppy years. He finally went to sleep under the house. It seemed like an eternity had passed since he was first presented to us as *the Horse you're having when you're not having a horse*.

Pa took it upon himself to look after the burial. Unfortunately, he couldn't decide on the most appropriate spot for his final resting-place. So Horse was dug up, plopped into the wheelbarrow and transported several times before he was finally allowed to rest in peace.

# Chapter Twenty Four

Before the curtain was to come down on the fifties, a few significant players were to make an entrance. For a couple of those, it was their debut on The Grand House stage. First, Cecelia moved back, permanently. This decision was predetermined by the death of Mrs. Wren. It was considered inappropriate for her to continue with the bachelor son her sole company. Cecelia was only in her late thirties when she exhibited symptoms of rheumatoid arthritis, with associated deterioration of the joints, especially her hands and feet. It was restricting her efficiency at the factory machines.

On her return to The Grand House, she and Patrice shared the second bedroom off the hallway. By this time, Patrice was well into her teens. Due to the decade between our ages, her recollections of the fifties are undoubtedly entirely different to mine.

The hairdressing apprenticeship she took, immediately after the death of our brother Russell, was relatively short-lived. Caustic perming solutions severely burnt her hands. Nevertheless, she experienced little difficulty finding alternative employment. I remember her job at the boiled-lolly factory because of a never-ending supply of Technicolor glucose in the kitchen jar. As one of the first *checkout chicks,* she became adept at the manual cash registers while working at the Brisbane Cash and Carry (the BCC) in the Valley. Most of these stores were ousted by the multinational supermarkets. Towards the end of her teenage years she worked in Perrott's Florist at Bowen Bridge, really handy to home.

Little Claude also moved effortlessly into the workforce after completing grade eight in 1955. He was bright and just the outgoing type employers warmed to. This enabled him to walk into a bicycle-selling job in Adelaide Street.

As a gregarious youngster, Little Claude naturally had an abundance of friends. When not at work, they hung out together at Rosemount.

Those who remember the Rosemount precinct of the fifties no doubt recall the charming old Eildon Post Office. It was opposite the then entrance to the Crystal Palace cinema. The nearby store proved a popular haunt with youngsters. This became abundantly evident after they introduced the latest fad from the U.S., a hamburger. (I couldn't for the life of me understand why there was never the least trace of ham.)

Whilst hanging around Rosemount, Little Claude struck up a friendship with a fellow five years his senior. The age difference between the parties to this burgeoning friendship wasn't in the least inhibiting, given Little Claude's candidly extrovert nature. Up against the taciturn manner of the other party, Ted, the contrast was almost Laurel and Hardy.

I could envisage the scenario where Little Claude rocked up to shoot off his mouth about his exploits. Ted was far too restrained or disinterested to tell him to bugger off. A unilateral truce was declared between the often-warring parties of Mighty Mouth and the combined forces of Big Ears and Noddy.

At the time of their first encounter, Ted was boarding with a family just a few doors up from the Crystal Palace. As the story of his life unfolded to Little Claude, it became increasingly evident why the guarded and withdrawn demeanour.

Life had been a mindless carnivore to this young man.

By the time he and Little Claude crossed paths, all he had left was vague memories of a family at Clayfield. He was the youngest of the bunch, abandoned by their mother when he had barely inched beyond babyhood. If that wasn't trauma enough, their father subsequently went to war never to be seen or heard of again.

With true bureaucratic compassion, the children were split up and assigned to various foster homes. Ted ended up in an orphanage somewhere near today's Wesley Hospital.

All contact with his siblings was lost, until he was old enough to leave the orphanage. At this juncture an elder brother, Bill managed to track him down. Having ascertained his brother's whereabouts Bill promptly secured him a carpenter's apprenticeship. Bill also had news about the rest of his family.

Ted's other brothers were now living interstate. His only sister had married a North Queensland cane farmer, of Italian stock and was now deeply committed to pasta and procreation up north.

I'm not sure why Ted didn't move in with Bill. It must have been a substantial reason. Having finally located his youngest brother, Bill kept a fraternal eye on him for the rest of his life. Bill was a wharfie. He had polio in his youth, the reason for his noticeable limp.

By the time Ted and Little Claude crossed paths at Rosemount, Ted had finished his apprenticeship and was working for a construction company.

Being the decade of Marlon Brando's *The Wild One,* it was nothing extraordinary to find Ted, like most other young blokes who hung round hamburger shops in the fifties, riding a motorbike. With the blossoming friendship between Little Claude and Ted, it naturally followed that Ted's friends became acquainted with Patrice and her friends and family. Before long, The Grand House was where the bikie gang congregated.

I vividly recall those Saturdays, even though I was still young enough to be getting under people's feet. There would be at least a dozen motorbikes neatly angle-parked outside the house. *Bodgees,* as they were tagged, literally hung off the verandahs. These young men, resplendent in their trademark stovepipe pants and leather jackets had hair slicked with great globs of Brylcream or Californian Poppy. Inside, their feminine counterpart, *Widgees* decked themselves in a uniform of peddle-pusher pants and flattering bare-midriff tops.

Occasionally, during these stylish gatherings Patrice or Little Claude would be prompted by the crowd to entice Neville Maroney to strut his stuff down the footpath in his mother's most glamorous frock and heels. Neville was never a drag when it came to screaming into theatrical action. At the first sound of clip-clopping from ill-fitting stilettos, a howl like a pack of rabid dingoes would issue from The Grand House.

As seniority would have it, the gatherings came to an abrupt halt when the Old Man arrived home unexpectedly early from the pub. He hit the roof on discovering the place overrun with teenage hooligans. With the exception of young Ted, for whom he had a soft spot, he advised the rest to bugger off in a way they couldn't refuse.

The Saturday afternoon soirées came to an abrupt end.

The Old Man also forbade Patrice to ride on the back of a motorbike. This didn't deter her one jot. However, the afternoon she came off and ended up with a broken ankle in hospital did slow her up some. Little Claude was still too young to have a motorbike. His adoring mother had, however, presented him with a pedal-bike. He could use this transport to and from work in town. This shiny new set of wheels was undoubtedly acquired on time payment. Ted was quietly amused to note that within a couple of weeks of receiving the gift, Little Claude had pulled it apart and repainted it.

As months went by, Ted was spending more time at The Grand House than he was at his boarding house. Everyone appeared comfortable with the arrangement. Whilst he never spoke with any animosity about the family he lodged with, isolated comments spoke volumes: such as there being butter on the table for the landlady's boys and only margarine for him.

Under such circumstances, it was inevitable Patrice and Little Claude would offer Ted a home at The Grand House, officially. Mum ran the idea by the Old Man and Paddy. Before we knew it, The Grand House had its next houseguest. Ted's impending arrival meant another room shuffle for mum to organise. It was while relocating Pa, from the front bedroom to one off the side verandah, that a shoebox fell off the top of the wardrobe.

Out came *The Last Will and Testament* of Patrick Fitzgerald.

This revealed Paddy's stipulation for The Grand House to pass to his three surviving children in equal shares.

I can't imagine how betrayed mum must have felt when it dawned on her that she had spent the better part of twenty years believing a lie. Surely, a torrent of questions flooded through her mind. Did her father *ever* have any intention of honouring the promise he made, all those years ago? Was that just a ploy to ensure she didn't move out when she married? Fergus was only eleven when she had tied the knot. She had already been his surrogate mother for several years by then. So, with or without Paddy's hollow promise, it would have been a heart-wrenching decision to abandon Fergus. Whilst it had been no real sacrifice for her to stay on; she couldn't deny her choice had impacted detrimentally on her marriage. (Living with his father-in-law had been difficult, to say the least. Had that untenable environment contributed to his excessive drinking?)

How different would things be, if only she had yielded to her husband's wishes and given herself over to marital bliss at New Farm? She put the document back into the box and proceeded with the task in hand, without mentioning the matter to anyone.

I was either six or seven (or at sixes and sevens) when all this was going on. Mum was expecting a baby! I was ecstatic at the prospect of having a new brother or sister. It was thrilling to know I was no longer to be the Bubba of the house. I doubt whether 'thrilled' would describe my mother's feelings at the prospect of gestation at thirty-nine. Her first-born was already seventeen.

In March of 1957, my baby brother came home. He quickly displayed a crop of curly ginger hair and an abundance of freckles. Ella wanted to call her new son Anthony but was put off by Claude's comment that you don't see red-headed Italians. (The unusual logic of this throwaway comment may have had something to do with the Roman, Mark Anthony, one and the same as swarthy screen-idol, Victor Mature in the Old Man's mind and the equally swarthy bunch residing at Caesar's house.)

It could also have had something to do with growing up close to the gasometers.

They agreed on Dan as a first name and Ted as a second. That must have made the new houseguest feel warmly accepted. The Grand House was now up to ten residents, not counting Horse and the stray cats Patrice continually enticed home.

With the rising occupancy rate, Ted's carpentry skills came in handy for enclosing the front and side verandahs. This style of renovation was being undertaken all over the district at a feverish pace. Anyone with shares in louvre-windows must have been raking it in. Who would have guessed that thirty years down the track, those same louvres once thought so stylish and fashionable, would be unceremoniously discarded with an air of abhorrence? Baby-boomers with a taste for renovation and a yearning for style and fashion, subsequently stripped the verandahs to their pristine glory.

# Chapter Twenty Five

The end of the fifties could best be described as the *Happy Days* era at The Grand House. Ted and Little Claude built a stockcar, which Ted raced on Saturday nights at the nearby Exhibition Speedway. Patrice and assorted friends would watch from Machinery Hill. The speedway was the hottest ticket in town. There would be no spot to throw down your blanket if you didn't arrive early. Always plenty of flashy action to keep the petrol-heads' A.D.D. focused on the oval - stockcars, speed cars, motorbikes and sidecars with impromptu entertainment in the interlude.

Three young brothers from Cribb Island were trying to kick-start a career in the music industry. The opportunity to perform in front of such a large, live audience must have been a lucky break. It earned speedway promoter of the day Bill Goode their undying gratitude. Rumour had it the boys created their band's name from the initials of the two Brisbanites instrumental in raising their profile. Bill Goode, of course, was one. The other was a hip disc-jockey, Bill Gates. It seems he too promoted them. Of course, that could have just been so much grandstanding. It makes more sense that 'Bee Gees' would stand for Brothers Gibb. Anyway, it served as a good illustration of the popular preference for delusion.

Back then, the Australian music industry was still in short bellbottoms. The stars most idolised were Americans such as Elvis Presley and Buddy Holly. Patrice and Ted jointly purchased the latest hi-fi unit. It was a beautifully finished rosewood cabinet, incorporating a radio and record player. Every Saturday morning, Patrice would pick up the latest 45 on her routine trips to the Valley. Saturday afternoons, music would blare from the cabinet as she ironed and starched her rope petticoats in readiness for the big night. 'The Purple People Eater' was one of my favourites.

Ted's musical taste inclined towards melancholy blues: he preferred artists such as Slim Whitman whose wistful melody, 'China Doll,' haunts me still (like a misplaced smell). Ted could also play a mean mouth organ. Unfortunately, whenever he did Horse would strike up howling like a lone wolf. Ted canned the mouth organ. What a zoo!

We still had the piano. The Old Man could belt out a rousing rendition of 'The Pub with No Beer,' (as long as there was enough beer for him to laugh about it). We had a drawer full of sheet music with titles such as 'The Wayward Wind' sung by Kay Starr (another misplaced smell). We had stacks of little *Songster* books providing the lyrics to various pop tunes.

All in all, a rousing song in my heart was aroused by the fiery musical atmosphere in which I resounded.

Saturday evenings meant us pranksterettes would toddle off to the Crystal Palace with mum. The Old Man would join us if he could still stand - or if we could still stand him.

I had already noticed how alcohol tends to bring out antagonisms. My earliest observations along these lines were of the Old Man. His belligerence was a constant source of embarrassment (if he joined us at the flicks). In those days, it was customary to play 'God Save the Queen' to initiate proceedings. The Old Man would refuse to join the crowd by standing for the anthem. He would sit sullenly whilst audibly muttering:

'She wouldn't stand for me!'

*I don't suppose too many would!* I thought to myself.

We generally timed our excursion to the flicks for the moment we heard Pa coming down the street from the Shamrock, singing:

'No more Chinamen allowed in New South Wales!'

This was another gem from his extensive repertoire of lyrics, ranging from the politically, through to the horribly incorrect.

At some point during the *Happy Days* era, Ted fell off his motorbike. While his injury was no more than a broken arm, the lethal possibilities that flashed before his mind's eye in those moments of helpless turmoil, wrought a decision to trade the bike in on something safer. That turned out to be an old, grey Mercury.

There hadn't been a motor vehicle at The Grand House since Pa laid the T-Model to rest all those years ago. Given his regular alcohol intake, he had mercifully neither desired nor had the finances to gamble with the lives of half of Brisbane by driving a lethal weapon.

The old, grey Merc will forever remind me of distressingly dreary Sunday drives to the Gold Coast. Mum, Royce, Dan and I would all squeeze into the back seat, early on Sundays. In those days it was a tedious trek along the old road to reach the Gold Coast, with an obligatory stop at Beenleigh to buy fresh bread for the picnic. To this day, I'll never understand why the decision-makers in our group always returned to the picnic spot at Greenmount.

As far as I was concerned, you're at the Gold Coast once you spot the ocean. So really, we could have been put out of our misery at Labrador. Unfortunately, old bozos don't pick up the wisdom of an eight-year-old too quickly. Thus, we kept on driving - past numerous inviting grassy knolls of laughing saltbush, sprayed over dreamy white sandy beaches inclining playfully down to the sighing surf.

We finally stopped in sight of the NSW border, my mind racked to a state of thunderous vertigo over the utter futility of it all.

Having spent the better part of the morning squashed and stifled in transit, there was barely enough time to set up, eat up and clean up before we had to pile it all back for the return journey. The woes of Royce and me were compounded by a dispiriting awareness of the ever-encroaching, unalterable progress of the next day. A school day. To top it all, Dan was invariably carsick at least once during these driving, driving, driving episodes.

After the old grey Mercury came the lilac-and-black Customline complete with fins and whitewall tyres. This was totally the coolest car in town. I don't recall any picnic outings in this vehicle, which is probably why I have fonder memories of it.

At the start of '58, Ted's twenty-first was looming. A select group of family and close friends was invited for a party on the side verandah, to celebrate his coming of age. As the day drew near, it was really no big secret: the occasion was also to break the news Ted would soon be a bona-fide member of the family.

The honour of announcing his first-born daughter's engagement to the houseguest fell to the Old Man. Unfortunately, he didn't make it back from the pub. So, it was left to Ted to be his own stand-in, clear his throat and do the honours.

Many an eyebrow jumped with the announcement that spinster Olive O'Shea from next door had pipped Patrice at the post in the race to the altar! She married none other than the Old Man's school-chum, Declan Murphy. The friendship between Declan and dad could be traced way back to Stratton Street. It was Declan's sister, Rose, who was responsible for Ella meeting Claude at that fateful dance in the Brisbane Restricted Sailing Club, many moons ago. Vast rivers had passed under the bridge since then.

By the time of Declan Murphy and Olive O'Shea's nuptials, both bride and groom were on the wrong side of forty. That minor objection wasn't going to hamper the bride's determination to indulge in a full-blown traditional wedding. After all, she had waited damn well long enough to snare a bloke. Declan was about the height of a pre-shrunk leprechaun and his intended looked up to him (physically, at any rate). Even wearing the latest in Dolly Varden headdresses, they could have taken their vows under a limbo stick without nudging the pole. In a wedding photo I glimpsed on their sideboard, long after the occasion I beheld a bride swathed in frills, flounces and furlongs of fabric. (It reminded me of a collapsed teapot cosy.)

I'm reliably informed I was at the wedding, although I can't recollect any of it. So I cannot in all honesty report whether he looked as though he knew what he was getting himself into. I rarely saw him smile in all the subsequent years we shared a side boundary. The man I remember barely drew breath - without first gauging his wife's tolerance of inhalation at that juncture.

After the marriage, Declan moved in next door with his antique bride, both her parents having passed away. Once more, dad and Declan were neighbours.

Yet, life wasn't about to re-create their carefree school-then-sailing days together in Stratton Street. Declan was now domestically groomed by bride. Dad eventually gave up on his old mate after one new-year's eve: he yelled an invitation over the fence for a quick celebratory drink up the Crown.

His wife yelled back that her husband wasn't allowed to go.

When her turn came to walk the aisle, Patrice also opted for a traditional wedding. After rigorously scouring the town's bridal shops, she settled on a beautiful, ballerina-length gown from Deon's. To compliment this, she chose a short veil and fashion-statement shoes with white pointy-toes and stiletto heels.

As a gangly ten-year old, I thought she looked utterly entrancing stepping into the wedding car, assisted by a proud and sober father. Mum made absolutely certain a photographer was on hand, to capture every single nuance of her daughter's marriage, at St Patrick's in the Valley. This was where, just over twenty years ago, she had tied the knot.

The small wedding party comprised a best man, a bridesmaid and me (as flower girl). I wore apricot and apple green. Instead of flowers, I carried a decorative parasol, which was presented to Nanny afterwards as a memento. Immediately after the 3 p.m. service a

Dimboola-style wedding breakfast was provided in an old wooden hall at Albion.

Everyone seemed to have sipped the golden nectar of joy that day. (Although I'm told Little Claude managed to get into a fight on the short tram-ride home.)

After a brief honeymoon at Kirra, the bride and groom returned to occupy the bedroom, which had last been Cecelia and Patrice's. The young couple purchased a handsome teak-veneer bedroom suite as an auspicious start to their married life. I couldn't help but marvel at how glamorous it looked, compared to the dowdy *His* and *Hers* suite still used by mum and dad.

Life soon became patterned by new routines at The Grand House. Patrice returned to her job at Perrott's Florists and Ted to his foreman's job at a building-site in town. Cecelia and I became room-mates on the side verandah, which remained the status quo for many years.

# Chapter Twenty Six

By 1960, television waves were irradiating Brisbane. For The Grand House opportunities for viewing were limited to peering through the electrical-store window, with half the neighbourhood jockeying for a spot. Not surprisingly, Mr. & Mrs. C. were the first in the street to acquire a set. They were usually the first to embrace new techno fads, having already had the electrical telephone installed. Being so good-hearted, it wasn't long before we were invited in to watch *Leave it to Beaver* on Sunday nights. In those days, viewing was limited to one station, broadcasting in black-and-white for a few hours each evening.

When Royce and I overheard Patrice and Ted discussing the pros and cons of purchasing a set, we could hardly contain our excitement. The acquisition of this latest box of flashing lights caused something of a quandary amongst the decision-makers. In the days when The Grand House was constructed, a lounge room would have been superfluous. Once again, Ted's building skills were called on to create a space where people could learn to relinquish their already limited communication skills.

The master bedroom became the lounge, after removing a section of wall between it and the dining room. Of course, this reduced the home to three bedrooms, with a shortfall. This was dealt with by re-partitioning the side verandah to create two sleep-outs. That left a small sunroom adjacent to the front door. Internal walls were coming down all over the neighbourhood as more aerials appeared on the skyline. That's why the remaining worker's cottages in the area now have only two bedrooms and a lounge.

A red lounge-suite appeared from out of the blue. I would hazard a guess it was on hire purchase. Furnished with the basics, evenings at The Grand House were soon to be bathed in the luminous gaze of the one-eyed monster. Without fail, it was viewed in total darkness just like the movies.

I was by now in year six at Windsor School. Fridays had taken on an exquisite dimension. As the last day of the school week, this glorious day already radiated a golden aura of freedom and release. Its supernatural qualities were now to be gilded by association with my favourite television shows, *The Texas Rangers, Sea Hunt* and *Seventy*

*Seven, Sunset Strip.* Before the electrifying *frisson* of Friday night's viewing, however, I now had therapy and exercise combined in Friday afternoon's dance class. (After I broke my leg, the physio suggested dancing.) Around the time this harmonic manner of recuperation was proposed, the new Waterside Workers' Club in Petrie Bight advertised ballet and tap classes for wharfie kids. Mum encouraged me to see if I would enjoy a disciplined frolic.

My foray into ballet and tap lasted just long enough to graduate from ballet slippers to toe shoes. Buying them must have put a decent-sized hole in the budget. The shoes had hardly been scuffed when, one afternoon, mum and I caught the Sandy Robertson TV Dance-Club segment on *The Channel Niner's Show.* The infectious beat, cheeky movement and flamboyant costumes - the essence of Latin-America - mesmerised me. I just *had* to join that conga line.

Maybe because the Old Man had been a bit of a twinkle-toes in his day, mum fancied at least one of his offspring ought to be able to hold her own on the dance floor. So, the ballet shoes were tossed from the carriage window, as I preferred ballroom dance classes on Friday afternoons. Mum would be waiting for me at the Harris Street tram stop when the big brass school bell peeled out *Freedom.* (It always sounded completely different in the afternoon).

She would accompany me to the community hall, on the corner of Broughton and Gympie Roads at Kedron. That hall - like so many of its kind *polka* dotting the neighbourhood in the first half of the twentieth century - has long since taken its last Tango. Since then, the site has been everything from a KFC, a fish 'n' chip shop through to a painter-and-decorator centre. It's a bit sad and pathetic when a community loses its dance. I still can't pass the site without thinking of Uncle George (Sandy Robertson's chief dance instructor in those days).

When Friday afternoon's classes were disbanded, mum and I ventured to the Ritz Ballroom in Petrie Bight, on Saturday mornings. My hobby had become invaluable to her as a social outlet. She chatted and laughed with parents arranged decorously along the edge of the dance floor. Their mouths would pool a general conversation while all eyes fixated on each *darling* tripping the light fantastic.

Before long, I had a dancing partner, Miles, whose parents owned a car. Mum and I were subsequently chauffeured to dances as far afield as Grafton. Miles fancied himself as a bit of a Don Juan when decked out in splendid regalia. His full-cut, frilly, ritzy cerulean satin-shirt might have come straight from Desi Arnez's dressing room.

Whilst the image enhanced his chances on the competitive dance floor; it did nothing for his street-side reception. When he made an inappropriate suggestion to one of the local lasses, she let him know what she thought of Cuban heels. (His left cheek turned as crimson as his cummerbund.)

The Old Man rarely involved himself with my girly hobbies, with one exception. The dancing studio sponsored a contingent from Brisbane to compete in championships at the Sydney Town Hall.

Parents and their primadonna offspring, baggage bursting to the seams with ball-gowns, satin-shirts and cummerbunds affrighted South Brisbane station. The train would be our overnight accommodation, as we travelled further than we had ever ventured. (I know for a fact, it was the first and last time the oldies went Sydney-side.)

It was the first time any of us had stayed in a hotel; this one was walking distance to Central Station. Three of us shared a room with a communal bathroom down the hall. The dining room downstairs was built to monumental proportions. I felt I would just get lost here in seething city throngs. I would end up another luckless statistic: a cipher amongst numbers that really counted.

Despite my earliest dancing costumes being homemade by Uncle Fergus's wife - the first pair of special soles coming at cost from a cobbler who lived opposite - my hobby must have consumed a largish dollop of The Grand House crème. This was undoubtedly the source of a deal of resentment from Patrice. Our relationship took some cool and defensive turns on the grisly and often contentious issue of dollops.

Tension was amplified by her newly diagnosed pregnancy. The young couple's double-income days were rapidly diminishing. Cream was coming off the menu altogether.

Towards the end of 1960, she and Ted produced a beautiful, blonde, blue-eyed boy. They laboured over a suitable tag for their pride and joy, eventually arriving at Bart. (A suave character from a black-and-white cowboy series called *Maverick*.)

How brainwashed we were by the constant bombardment of American culture through movies and television! Our heroes had names like Bronco, Bat (Masterton) and Wyatt (Earp). I put my two-bob's worth in, suggesting they call the baby Rowdy (Yeates). This was the young Clint Eastwood, who played a starring rôle in Rawhide (my contemporary idol). Luckily for my new nephew, my opinion was ignored – as usual.

We worshiped these founding fathers of Marlboro country, where nothing *usual* ever happened. The only people who worked for a living were the sheriff and the bartender. Being sheriff was the biggest joke in town, as he was bound to get shot (often by the hero). Bartenders rarely outlasted a series. Women were either piano players or whores. Nobody ever went to the toilet. We all dreamed this great American dream, where *getting even* with a gun oozed with sexy heroism in tight pants. (You have to wonder what happens to all that subliminal information.)

So, Patrice's job at Perrott's Florist became nipped in the bud by the bub.

Around the same time Cecelia, then forty, was finally coerced onto the invalid pension by arthritis. Paddy was an aged pensioner. (This was before Gough Whitlam addressed the iniquitous discrepancy between pensions and the cost of living.)

The Old Man managed to hold down his job as a wharfie, although his number-one priority remained booze, ever to the attrition of the household purse. If it wasn't upsetting enough for mum - his barely handing over sufficient to feed and clothe his family - he sometimes compounded her woes by losing her meagre purchases.

One time, mum, packed out like a department-store Santa with dilly-bags full of household necessities was jostling with mixed results against crowds in the Valley. In desperation, she sought the Old Man out at one of his regulars. He took a couple of bags, with the promise to follow on the next tram - soon as he finished his drink. He turned up hours later, completely soused minus the bags.

Out of this bleak financial situation, mum and Patrice hatched a desperate remedy. Both had bonny bouncing babies so it was difficult to resist the 'Big Bucks for Infants' Internal Organs' offer by a private hospital. (Just kidding!) It seemed a duplication of tasks: two home-makers and child-carers, when one could be out working.

Mercifully, Patrice drew the short straw and returned to work.

I say this because her incompetence in the kitchen could only be matched by an anorexic zombie with a bad attitude and, of course, my own. I shuddered to think what might have passed for an evening meal, had their rôles been reversed.

She applied at the factory at the end of the street and never looked back. Meantime, Ella became surrogate mother to her eighteen-month grandson, who was raised like a brother to her son of barely five years.

# Chapter Twenty Seven

Patrice made a decision considered 'modern' for a young woman of the day, to be a driver. Around that time, Little Claude purchased his first motorbike against the wishes of his father. Ted moved from lilac-and-black Customline celebrity status to a more functional Ford. He subsequently became a dyed-in-the-wool Ford man, delivering the full tribal fan-dance of scoffing at anyone foolish enough to contemplate Holdens, Japanese or European cars.

As time went by, the Old Man's drinking routine became ever less punctuated by periods of work. His moonlight flits to the Hotel Watch House turned a bit regular. When he found himself *behind* bars instead of *at* one, he would use his phone-call entitlement to *pleeeease Patrice* into collecting him. This tradition began to bug Little Claude to the point where he declared it was cruel-to-be-kind time.

On this particular morning, when the anticipated call rang the house awake at an unholy hour - the Old Man having been missing the night - Little Claude announced he would take charge of proceedings and any proceedings of the charge. With that, he jumped on his bike and sped to his mission of mercy in the direction of town.

It seems the Old Man was somewhere between tentative and a gibbering wreck at the prospect of climbing on the back, especially in his delicate condition, especially with a motocross-hoon driver with more speeding tickets than dropped bikes to his credit.

Little Claude took off like a bat out of hell (his preferred start). The tighter the Old Man's grip, the faster he went. That was the last time the Old Man phoned from the watch house. His return moods were subsequently much chastened by a tram-ride (he looked terribly unwell). The occasional long walk home didn't noticeably manifest the purported health benefits, either. He looked like a chewed up bit of string when he stumbled in the door.

Soon after that, Little Claude had a nasty spill from his bike in Grafton Street, with his imagination spilling even more gory possibilities. Like Ted before him, it was enough to fillip him into transport with less image and more wheels.

Having finished with school after year eight, Little Claude furthered his education at night classes. By 1963, he had already been awarded his Senior Certificate. To celebrate his twenty-first birthday, in July that year a party was thrown at The Grand House. He invited all his mates. Some of these blokes were straight out of the *Arfur* Daley school of freelance entrepreneurs. There was one in particular who, despite tender years, had the dubious distinction of having been banned from every racetrack in Australia. Don't think for one second I would reveal why (even if I knew!)

Around this time, Little Claude changed jobs to a motor spare-parts salesman, much to the disappointment of the man who had given him his first job (and who tried several times to coax him back). The appeal of his new job wasn't just the handier location, being walking distance to The Grand House but the drop-dead gorgeous, blue-eyed blonde receptionist.

Little Claude and Jenny shared an interest in Australian Rules football, which Little Claude had now been playing, quite successfully, for several years. He played for Uncle Fergus's old club, which had amalgamated with Zillmere to be known as the Windsor-Zillmere Football Club. Little Claude was a dedicated player who had already won an A-Grade, 'Best and Fairest' trophy.

He and Jenny both had to overcome several abortive situations with their respective families, in the gestation stages of their relationship. For their part, Jen's parents didn't fancy the idea of their pin-up, only daughter choosing a swarthy, olive-skinned footballer they considered *a bit Mediterranean.*

For mum's part, the mere idea of her precious firstborn son being seduced from the nest by this cheap, stuck up, bottle-blonde tart was abhorrent. Of course, she was way off the mark on all four counts when it came to the sweet and lovely Jennifer Nosworthy. It was blatantly obvious to everyone that mum was blinded by fear . . . fear of anyone stealing her son. Mum was so *endearingly* reluctant for any of her darlings to fly the nest.

The hail of verbal compost from both sides did nothing but encourage Little Claude and Jen's relationship to blossom. It wasn't long before his studies paid dividends: he was offered a well-paid junior-executive position with a sizeable and successful company. It was a wonderful opportunity, financially and vocationally with just one drawback: the vacancy was in Townsville.

Jen and Little Claude had an engagement party at the Hamilton Library Hall before Little Claude headed north, alone, to take up his new position.

Jen remained in the spare-parts salesroom, keeping herself busy with wedding preparations until Little Claude returned briefly in February '66 to tie the knot, at St. Michael and All Angels Church in New Farm.

I was sixteen by then and chuffed to be included in the wedding party. I wore a long, blue gown fitted under the bust (which I didn't have at that stage). The celebration at a reception lounge in Bowen Hills was so lavish: it must have set Jen's parents back a wad or two. They married the same week decimal currency was introduced. Everyone talking about money at the time the parents were being relieved of so much of it must have abetted their angst no end.

Immediately following their wedding, Little Claude and Jen drove to Townsville in their newly acquired, secondhand Vauxhall Viva.

The choice of wife met with Ted's approval but the same could not be said for those wheels.

# Chapter Twenty Eight

By the time of Little Claude's marriage, I had rung up more nine to fives than a cashier on speed.

Digressing for a moment to the end of 1960, while in year six at Windsor State School, there was a recruitment drive around the neighbourhood conducted by the Catholic parish priest. The upshot was, mum ran it by Royce and me about swapping over to the Catholic school to complete our primary education. Considering his inherently devil-may-care nature, the riot of objections issuing from this sudden preference-oriented, discriminating Royce was mind-boggling.

It was a moot point, anyway. At the first opportunity Royce threw off his shackles to escape the school system forever. He turned fourteen in January and was liberated by May. The mastermind behind his successful bid for freedom was Mr. C. He secured his young mate Smiley a factory position in the Valley, where he had worked for many years. Errol-John was already on the payroll, courtesy of his father.

This left me formulating a vague plan of somehow ingratiating myself with Mr. C. to entice him to make it a threesome. I was well aware the scheme had some minor flaws – like my age and incompetence. I was still fine-tuning those annoying details in my mind, as I moved across the street to the opposition camp, as it was known.

In those days, holders of the moral high-ground were split into two distinct blocs. Factions of the faithful were 'Filthy Micks' and *the others*, 'Proddy Dogs'. Chilling the way religion polarises people from a tender age. Thank god for atheists! No wonder John Lennon wrote wistfully of an idyllic world devoid of religion. . . . *Imagine!*

I had been ambivalent about changing schools. I certainly felt no sentimental attachment to Windsor State. There was never any thought given to a new learning environment perhaps stimulating creative thinking. (That sort of deliberation was well outside our received information.) It was only when a school chum, Rosemary was approached in the same recruitment drive, we decided to grit our teeth and bear it for the shared adventure.

Rosemary was one of scant allies during my school plight. Not that I was anti-social - I just didn't fancy spending precious spare time with anyone not wholly committed to educational anarchy. Rosemary was a rare exception, as Sharon had been a few years earlier.

It was Sharon's mother who had helped Patrice into a hairdresser's apprenticeship, after Russell's death. Sharon and I had been good playmates back then. We would have remained so, had her family not moved to Ferny Grove. I recall taking the train once to visit her, after the move. The unadulterated luxury of her new place, toilet and bathroom inside *and* hot running water at the turn of a tap had me all *oohs* and *aahs*. Laminex glowed atop kitchen surfaces and the stove didn't need wood. Sharon had her own bedroom, complete with a built-in wardrobe. The surrounding houses were almost identical, apart from colour variations to the exterior. They all looked wonderful compared to the shambling old wreck I called home.

As is so often the case, Sharon and I lost contact after her move. My closest friend was now Rosemary.

If I thought the state system was intimidating, a whole new dimension was added to the word at this Catholic place. At least the teachers at my old school bore some vague resemblance to normal people (however otherworldly their behaviour). The eerie figures that silently stalked the creaking, wooden corridors of my new Alma Mater kept threatening to take me to their leader. Every inch of their person was concealed under flowing robes. Their face was encased in a stiff white frame, the only visible section being between eyebrows and chin, like someone looking back at you through a letterbox. I could swear they floated on air, balletic, as though in midst performance of *Penguin Lake,* wafting in and out of classrooms without so much as a ripple in their wake.

Embarrassment was added to intimidation when I was placed with the year ones for religious instruction, because my knowledge of two-millennia old Middle Eastern superstitions wasn't up to scratch. I accepted there was nothing to go back to across the road and progressed to year eight in 1962 - secure in my newfound wisdom that God made the world in six days and Darwin was a heretic who should have been burned at the stake. Nothing like a good solid grounding in rationalism to win me a scholarship! My question 'Any chance God renovates houses as a sideline?' didn't get serious consideration.

That was to be the final year any scholarship exam would be conducted in Queensland. From '63 onwards, students would compulsorily proceed to high school on the successful completion of year seven, thus eliminating the option of bailing out at the end of year eight. Up till then, it wasn't uncommon for girls who left school after scholarship either to proceed to the workforce, or undertake a stint at a commercial college, if they aspired to an office job. Either way, employment was guaranteed because work was in abundance.

Towards the end of year eight, I made the unlikely decision to study for the final exam. I was acting out of my part here, motivated solely by the fear of appearing in *The Courier Mail* as a failure - where scholarship results were exposed for the world to see. Hurricane sighs of relief shot through my curtains, the morning my dance partner dropped by with his parents and with the paper.

I passed!

Mum was so delighted she resolved this warranted sending me to high school (after little or no consultation with me). I was first in the family to walk the bookish path. I felt hesitant about breaking new ground as an academic pioneer. I had seen enough Westerns to know that pioneers end up with an arrow in the seat of knowledge. Given different circumstances, Little Claude would have seized the opportunity to continue his full-time education. He was far more the academic type. Our erstwhile penury prevented any chance he might have had of full-time high school education. I suppose it was a case of being born at the wrong end of the bunch.

Mum's decision to send me on to high school might have been based on her feeling that I lacked the crusty wherewithal to tackle the commercial world.

By divine grace, the cost of fees at even a second-string Catholic high pre-empted any option to continue. So, in January 1963, I walked through the gates of the relatively new Kelvin Grove High School. The decision-makers at The Grand House were probably influenced by the reputation of Kedron High (considered back then to be a tad rambunctious).

It must have set mum back a fortune to deck me out in the daggy, long, pleated, green skirt uniform with a baggy white blouse (lacking the body particulars to stretch the higher button-holes). Then there were the gloves and the red-and-green striped tie accessories to be worn at all times in public. If that wasn't humiliation and torment enough, gruesome grey stockings wrinkled around my shapeless legs (because my non-existent hips couldn't support a suspender belt). Having already banished us to the sartorial wilderness, there were loathsome black shoes, throwbacks to some puritan era when 'functional and sensible' ruled okay. To top off the scarecrow accoutrements, there was the summer straw-hat and the winter green beret with a red bow fetchingly stuck on one side.

Mum had the additional outlay of a sport's uniform. This really was an absolute and total waste, considering my athletic ineptitude was matched only by my loathing of any type of sport. Books were a further expense, and the special Esterbrook pen for shorthand. Like most girls, I was enrolled in the Commercial Course focusing on office skills like shorthand, typing and bookkeeping. Boys were generally directed towards the Manual Arts Course.

The effort in passing scholarship had so exhausted me, I settled into my old skiving habits, which soon saw me relegated to a class of dysfunctionals and under-achievers. One teacher trudged into our class of ne'er-do-wells, approached the blackboard and wrote the words: *The Good Die Young - 3C3 Will Live Long,* insisting we type it a hundred times. She then walked out.

Miraculously, I passed year nine and was therefore able to make a comeback in '64 to see how year ten would turn out. As the junior examination loomed, I became increasingly agitated about the prospect of failure. Finally, in desperation, I made the life-altering decision to jump ship and find a job - before everyone else did likewise. Being wholly ill-equipped to cope with the commercial world had barely entered my mind. Mum was devastated: I had delayed announcing my intention until after she paid the king's ransom demanded to sit exams.

I scanned the 'Positions Vacant; Women and Girls' section of *The Courier Mail* until my eyes fell on an ad for a junior at a real-estate office in Chermside. I ducked up to the local phone box, called and was interviewed that day. I was so nervous confronting the two partners, everything was a blur - apart from remembering to leave the phone number of Mr. & Mrs. C. up the street.

Mr. & Mrs. C. were always generous about things like that.

A call came the next day. It enabled me to escape the heat of academia and jump headfirst into the workforce, without so much as a second thought as to what rocks or flotsam lay in wait.

I was just confused, naïve, fourteen and *at sea*.

# Chapter Twenty Nine

Before pursuing my brilliant career, it might be opportune to note a couple of somewhat capricious events at The Grand House. This was whilst I was still officially 'at' high school. Although I continue to refer to the house as grand, by then it was anything but. If it once felt like a clipper in a sea of barges, it now looked like it had sailed through the Bermuda Triangle once too often. Its days of glory were emblazoned on our memories. They were its last reserve.

Apart from Ted's past handiwork - partitioning rooms for essential sleeping quarters - there had been no serious expenditure on maintenance since the place was built in the twenties. The imposing front staircase had long since fallen victim to wear and tear and had been replaced by a mediocre set running parallel to the house. By now, these too, were rickety. The weatherboard exterior hadn't been anywhere near a paintbrush and the roof was rusted and leaking in several places. Little trace remained of the stylish coloured glass; it resembled a masking-tape roadmap, covering webs of cracks. Many sash-windows had to be propped open with pieces of wood, the stays having collapsed. The entire structure inclined noticeably toward one corner of the front verandah.

The bathroom remained in its original Spartan condition. With the advent of sewers, the WC from way up the backyard had been relocated to the bottom of the tottering, rear steps. This contraption had a chain attached to a rusting seesaw lever atop a metal tank perched over your head. Because it always seemed to be leaking, my post-evacuations traumas centred on groping around in the semi-lit wet for toilet paper. Ah, the sweet bouquet of last-week's newspaper, torn into uneven strips and hung from a nail by a loop of old string. Selecting the right politician's face on the newsprint for the cleanup job has indelibly rendered the thunder box a metaphor for the ballot box.

All these shortcomings became magnified as homes around the neighbourhood were energetically renovated. Trendsetters bricked in their unders and extended the back to incorporate indoor bathrooms and toilets. Some splashed out on the fashionable 'patio'.

There had been a few grudging concessions to modern technology at The Grand House. Gas lighting had been scantily

95

replaced by electricity: the only power points were in the kitchen and lounge. So none of the bedrooms had ready access to electricity and none of the sleep-outs had overhead lighting. Cooking was all on the wood stove; the copper boiler was our only source of hot water for bathing and laundering for some time. We had, at least, upgraded the Mawson ice-chest to a larger, metallic one - although no less reliant on daily ice deliveries.

Eventually, a little bow-fronted Crossley refrigerator took on the chilling task. Further down the track, a washing-machine appeared. These mechanised housewives were threatening to throw women out of domestic work and onto the dole all over Australia. To power it, a hole had to be made through the floor so a lead could be run to the power-point in the kitchen. Considering the troops mum laundered for (Windsor Zillmere football jerseys and all) the washing machine must have amounted to her first inanimate romance.

It was a weird and wonderful journey into techno skullduggery for us. A round tub with its own agitator doing *let's twist again*. Attached to the rim of this great bowl were two rollers, enclosed and on a pivot. This enabled them to be swivelled over the machine's tub or the nearby concrete washtubs. Once the clothes had become as interwoven as their constituent yarn, it was a matter of pivoting the rollers then setting them to devour mode. Hand feeding clothes from the tub through crushing rollers was a slow, sloppy, squeezy, drippy process, which was repeated for the rinse cycle. It looks cumbersome today (but then washing with water will soon be archaic). It was a quantum leap from the stone-age, wood-fired copper boiler, which mum used to stuff with clothes before cudgelling them with a big stick until they were bullied into giving up the dirt.

Given the occupants' apparent dedication to dereliction as an ambient motif, it was a wonder anyone except diehard fans of *The Addams Family* would voluntarily choose The Grand House. So, I was surprised to learn of Uncle Fergus's decision to resume his residence, together with his wife and two sons. I gather it was an interim arrangement while selling acreage at Mt. Cotton and finding some alternative. I was far too flighty at 13 to go losing my kaleidoscopic mind in that humongous grey-zone of adult money matters.

We already had quite a houseful *before* Fergus and entourage. The only available space was the small, enclosed sunroom at the front. Somehow, into this confined area they squeezed a double bed and a double bunk. The arrival of the cousins coincided with the departure of the wood-stove. Uncle Fergus and his wife funded a new, gas, upright Chef.

All things considered, with so many parties residing under the one roof this new arrangement appeared to meld without melée. There was some friction, after I complained to mum about the run-and-fetch routine to the shop, instead of my cousins - who were *busy studying*.

In truth, they probably were. As far as I knew, that was the excuse you used when you couldn't be bothered to think up an excuse. There was never any genuine animosity toward my cousins. I felt sorry for them. (Anyone who ranked a D or an F in excuses could depend on my utmost condescending regard.) Not only were they crammed into impossibly restrictive sleeping quarters, their mother insisted they read Bible passages every day. Having never completely recovered from my close-encounter with Christianity, the thought of systematic indoctrination by the religion that brought you the Holy Inquisition, gave me a nervous tic.

We did our best to cohabit congenially in crowded conditions, little suspecting the strange fate rounding the corner, in the shape of a Ranch Wagon towing a sizeable caravan. Mum answered the front door to an affable chap with a hint of European accent. He enquired after Ted, introducing himself as his brother-in-law from North Queensland. Next, he indicated the vehicle and caravan outside, bulging with wife and family.

They were between seasons on the cane farm - taking the opportunity to catch up with his wife's long-lost siblings. Their ultimate destination was some obscure interstate location but they were hoping to spend a couple of days with Ted, *en route*.

Mum politely agreed to this polite request as the vehicle and van were already rolling down the side-lane into the backyard. I lost count at ten as to how many emerged. All shapes, sizes, ages and genders ranging from a babe in arms to a girl who looked not much older than me.

It must have been maddening on the road to Brisbane with such a sizeable assembly in tow, all taking it in turns to whine: *How much longer before we get there?* They were overjoyed at the opportunity to stop for awhile and stretch their legs. That joy turned to exuberance when they heard the recently opened Centenary pool complex was just up the road and the Exhibition tenpin-bowl, nearby.

After that, the parents had absolutely no chance of enticing their clan back into that vehicle to go bush. So they camped in the backyard for what seemed like eons. The headcount around the place was about twenty-five. Their eldest daughter becoming my good friend compensated for the claustrophobia.

Spag. bol. made its debut as part of our staple diet, which until then had been monotonous mutton and three predictable veg. The chef of the moment decided to boil the spaghetti in the copper, in the backyard. Radiant white spaghetti was something else. Not long after that, Uncle Fergus and his family moved on to Bracken Ridge.

These events slipped by just as I was about to step onto the treadmill of working life.

# Chapter Thirty

The transition from school to paid work was a crooked learning curve. My real-estate employers at Chermside must have been devastated by my incompetence at purportedly school-taught skills. I wished I had paid more attention during the shorthand and bookkeeping lessons and practiced the manual Olivetti typewriter more diligently. All I remember clearly from high school were the magnificent purple jacarandas lining Gilchrest Avenue, as I gazed out of the classroom window. A teacher's dire warning used to ring in my ears:

*If you haven't started studying for finals by the time the jacarandas are in bloom, you're a certainty to fail.*

They even managed to ruin the brilliantly iridescent purple patches of fallen jacaranda petals in spring!

I tried to steady my nerves, reminding myself it was their gamble, employing a young, inexperienced girl on a low wage. The gambler in them no doubt reckoned me more of a shoo than a shoo-in for Lady Luck by this stage. I turned fifteen in two months, so I was entitled to a raise.

That quickly drew matters to a head. They determined to cut their losses by suggesting I look elsewhere for employment.

You could stumble over any doorstep, fall flat on your face and still get taken on in those days. I fell into my second job at the first attempt. This success was in part attributable to the glowing reference from my first employers. I was again the office junior in a dull, conservative and well-established real estate firm in Queen Street.

Here, I found my old friend Sharon! We had lost contact after her family moved to Ferny Grove. She was also working for a real-estate office in the Valley when our paths crossed at Errol-John's wedding. Our respective families witnessed some petite, dark-haired beauty from New Farm become his wife.

During our conversation at the Oddfellows-Hall reception, I got the feeling Sharon enjoyed a more adventurous lifestyle than me. She was already used to riding the train from Ferny Grove to the bright lights on Friday and Saturday evenings. She liked places where there was ample opportunity to meet men. I took up her invitation to stay over, one weekend, so we could hit the hotspots together.

Sharon had freckles and long, red, curly hair. She disliked the curls so much she had to iron out the least trace of curvature before we could leave. By the time the hair was presentable, we had become increasingly less so. I'm not sure where we went, how we got there or who in their right mind could have allowed us in, but I distinctly recollect a Stomp Pit.

We lost contact again. I heard on the grapevine that she had married a fellow from Ipswich. It's on the same line as Ferny Grove, so it might have been a railway romance.

Meanwhile, back at my second attempt to brave real-estate office junior, I was just managing to hold my own, running between the post office and bank when fate struck again.

The head girl at this place - an ice princess with perfectly groomed attitude and lemon-sucking mouth - decided I should volunteer for the switchboard during lunch hour. The apparatus necessitated plugging cords into a socket board, with a dozen or so incoming lines and extensions too numerous to count. Coming as I did, from a home without the latest in telephonic technology, this seemed to threaten some user's foreknowledge.

The fragile confidence I had built like a house of cards to deal with the corporate world, collapsed. This time, I resolved to jump before being pushed. Once again, with relative ease, I started as an office junior with an American manufacturing company close to Stratton Street, in Newstead. Barely eleven months ago, I had turned my back on Kelvin Grove High and already I was starting my third job.

This was certainly a case of third time lucky. I have a bouquet of rosy memories for this working period. Not only was the workload a cinch, but the social side was congenial.

Exhilarated by life, I started to exercise. I decided to walk to work along Campbell Street as an alternative to changing trams in the Valley. Fortunately, however, a couple of days later, a guy in the office who regularly took that route saw me.

Only seconds before my exercise routine became monotonous, I had a daily lift to and from the office in a cool, British, racing-green sports car. After twelve months or so I was promoted to switchboard operator and felt totally competent using the very equipment that had once reduced me to a quivering technophobe.

Every year, their Social Club dinner danced at a swanky venue, like the Skyline Room in the National Hotel. We all dressed to the nines. I cajoled mum into running up a long, swish evening gown on the pedal-powered Singer. It was a replica of some ritzy number Dusty Springfield sported on *Bandstand*. Naturally, I had no idea of the colour, TV being black-and-white. Every tiny detail of my fave, rave pop-singer's outfit was imprinted on my mind's eye. It took untold hours to sew the crystal and pearls onto the bodice and sleeves.

Patrice was no Cinderella, either. She and Ted regularly attended the Speedway Ball. Invariably, she would purchase a new Grace Kelly-style gown with off-the-shoulder flyaway, chiffon scarves.

There was always rivalry between sisters back then. This was never more evident than when I was competition dancing. Mum ran up a sleek costume of gold fabric for an important event on my dancing calendar. I spent the morning at a beauty salon having my hair tinted red, then piled high on my head. I even went as far as having a full makeover including glitter eye-shadow.

'Look at lambykins dressing up as mutton!' snarled Patrice.

My appearance was a constant niggle. Shoulder blades protruded out of my back further than my undeveloped chest protruded from my front, giving the impression my torso was the wrong way round. I craved the petite Judy Stone proportions of my sister. Having to disguise my 5 feet 8 inch elevation and underdeveloped stature was humiliating. It was humiliating just to feel humiliated about something as unfixable as body parts.

I took heart for awhile when supermodel Twiggy burst onto the fashion scene. Suddenly, being a lanky scrawny waif was in vogue. This solace was short-lived, however. A glance down the small print of a magazine article on my short-term saviour revealed the depressing truth. While I was her height, Twiggy was actually heavier. My niggling self-esteem gauge was teetering in the anorexic red-zone. Family and neighbours who could have stepped straight off the set of *Darby O'Gill and the Little People* compounded the quandary. It afforded cold comfort to overhear I had taken after Rebecca, also a tall lady.

I developed a noticeable stoop. Mother took steps to rectify this by sending me to the Dorothy Bourke Salon of Elegance. Here I was to learn techniques for walking with books balanced on my head in order to appear refined. (Either that or they were training us to compete with performing seals.) I was gorged with the finer points of etiquette and good breeding. Anyone who knows me today would concede that this expenditure had been a somewhat misguided investment.

I did have one admirer in those times. Karl was a workmate of Royce's. He spent most, if not all, his spare time at The Grand House.

Karl, like Ted before him, sought refuge from a dysfunctional home. Reading between the lines, it seems Karl's father was an alcoholic, with one significant difference to our resident soak. Whilst the Old Man daily reddened our cherubic faces to a subtle hue of beetroot, he never once laid a hand on any of us.

This was not the case with Karl's father.

Although Karl was Royce's friend, he would regularly buy me embarrassingly extravagant gifts (considering our relationship was platonic). One birthday, he presented me with a Wallace Bishop Loyal watch. As pleasant and attentive as Karl was, I couldn't possibly take seriously someone who revered Elvis Presley to the extent of fashioning his hair in His image.

After all, I had close family ties to one of The Beatles.

# Chapter Thirty One

Royce's attention during the sixties remained firmly fixed on horses. They were a necessary therapy after his daily dose of stultification at the factory. He would trudge uncomplainingly to work, Monday to Friday in his overalls and steel-capped boots. Come Saturday, there would be a complete metamorphosis.

Virtually out of his first week's pay, he bought himself a slick, black suit and a pair of the latest in black, pointy-toe leather shoes. Decked out in this finery, topped with a racecourse-tout's hat and binoculars professionally slung from the neck (a cumbersome accessory) he could be seen heading uphill toward the trams for Ascot or Doomben.

The trams were a sheer delight for all of us at The Grand House. As youngsters we loved riding them Sunday afternoons; there was so much release and freedom in their determined motion and it was wonderful sightseeing. (Letting the scenery slide past as if you were detached from it.) Lovingly maintained flowerbeds used to border the tracks from Lutwyche Cemetery to the Chermside Terminus.

Everyone hopped on trams. Saturday mornings it was standing-room only for the Valley. Ladies would don their better frocks, often amplifying the gilded lily theme with matching hat and gloves.

The Valley rivalled the town as a retail centre, boasting three major department stores - McWhirter's, T.C. Beirne's and Waltons as well as specialty shops. G.J. Coles & Co were for the budget-conscious with no less than two outlets, anatomically distinguished as 'Top Coles' and 'Bottom Coles'. Naturally, wherever Coles opened, Woolworths would soon be next. This was the case in the Valley.

We tend to take for granted extended trading hours these days. It wasn't so long ago *weekend shopping* was the last three hours of Saturday morning. This meant confronting utter chaos for some, scurrying from store to store jostling the throng. The most popular meeting spot was under the McWhirter's clock. (You would be amazed who could be standing there on Saturday mornings!)

With marathon expertise, Patrice could manage the hairdresser, deposit lay-buys at several stores and throw in a quick rummage through the bargain basement at McWhirters all between 8.30 and 11.30

a.m.! Had they awarded degrees for shopping skills, my sister would have graduated *cum laude*.

For my thirteenth birthday, mum apologised for having brought me into this world by giving me a portable record player, in partial recompense. It certainly became my favourite form of escapism. This started an intensely *now* activity - the Saturday morning browse through the record sections of department stores. I had several LPs by the hip music sensation, Herb Alpert and the Tijuana Brass.

At 11.30 a.m. sharp, shop doors were firmly barred to mindless acquisition and it was usually at around 11.29 that I would suddenly remember the record I just had to have.

We then scrambled back onto the trams piled up like bag ladies on the move. Bart and Dan were usually waiting at our hop-off point to greet their respective mothers. They knew there would be a surprise in a dilly-bag, such as a matchbox car or a capgun.

The desirability of capguns diminished dramatically for Dan after one Guy Fawkes' night. He was a sprightly lad, frolicking around the backyard with his trusty toy gun in hand and a roll of replacement caps in his back pocket.

He happened to drop to the ground on his backside, exactly where a spent cracker-paper lay. Unfortunately, the paper hadn't burnt out. The residual heat fired the gunpowder in his pocket and set his pants ablaze. Little Claude pushed his terrified younger brother onto the grass to extinguish the searing. But the caps continued to explode.

Poor Dan ended up with a messy scar like chewing gum stretched over his left 'gloot' (as they say in the aerobic ads.). It was around this time that Guy Fawkes' night was banned and firework displays subsequently became the exclusive domain of licensees like Rick Birch. I don't *think* the two incidents were related. Corner-store operators would have felt the pinch: sales of all types of crackers used to go like a rocket right through October up to the fifth of November.

The older boys, including Little Claude, Royce and Errol-John stocked up on Penny Bungers and Tom Thumbs to execute all the usual stunts designed to maximise noise and threat levels. Tom Thumbs under a saucepan or Penny Bungers in a letterbox were effective. Letterboxes could be blown right off the fence. What brilliant minds can discover! Interesting reactions could be elicited from unsuspecting motorists, by throwing a bunger down a drain. It had to explode exactly as the vehicle passed to produce the full impromptu, heart-attack scenario. By the time

Bart and Dan were schoolboys, Guy Fawkes' nights had become a distant memory of smouldering gloots.

The two boys grew up more like brothers than uncle and nephew. Hardly surprising, considering their parity in years. Because Ella was grandmother to one, and mother to the other, someone, somewhere came up with a nickname for her. That name was 'Dearie' and it stuck ever since.

*Dearie* escorted both boys on the lengthy walk to Windsor School every morning. She would be waiting at the gate when the bell rang in the afternoon. She embraced tuckshop duty enthusiastically - with silver teaspoons from Windsor Primary and Kedron High testifying to her dutiful service. Bart and Dan's school-related activities must have replaced my dancing soirées as her social outlet.

I had reached the painfully self-conscious hormonal stage of blushing to have mother tag along with me to class.

Bart and Dan engaged in typically sixties boys' stuff, like billycart racing. The Grand House was ideally sited, being at the bottom of two hills. They christened their homemade contraption the Rolls Canardly: although it *rolls* easily down the hill it *can hardly* be pushed up again (due to the quantity of optional extras hanging off it). The track down either hill to the side-gate finish-line was fraught with formidable dangers. I don't necessarily refer to the chance of a spill. The boys needed to be constantly vigilant when it came to passing *Mrs. Rheem's* house.

The Rheem tag was because she threw hot water over them, should their cart swerve across her impeccably mown nature-strip. If Mrs. Rheem was 'coming on too hot and strong' (a commercial-TV shibboleth of the day) they would prefer the alternative track.

The change of track was, however, frequently met with a vehement ear bashing from the spinsters at the top of the hill - about wearing out the asphalt on their footpath or something.

# Chapter Thirty Two

In January 1967, Royce felt little other than fear and loathing for his upcoming twentieth birthday. The Vietnam War was headlined daily and twenty-year olds faced the horrific prospect of being drafted into the fray, through a compulsory national service scheme.

Mum's worst fears were realised when Royce was notified to start basic training in August. Karl missed the ballot. He may have felt a tinge of regret about that. A pre-existing kidney condition probably would have eliminated him at the medical, anyway.

What already started as a bugger of a year, soon got considerably worse when the rains came. By the eve of the Queen's Birthday long-weekend it had been deluging for weeks. Surveying the daily downpour was particularly depressing for a work colleague at Newstead, who had scheduled her wedding for the Saturday afternoon. What a way to take the plunge!

Floods at The Grand House weren't news. In my childhood, whenever high tides coincided with heavy rains, the water regularly crept up the street from the creek to submerge one or two steps. Back then, it was exciting splashing about in a watery playground. Mind you, we never swam in the murk. (I couldn't swim to save myself.) We kids contented ourselves with wading until the waters receded, then slopping up mud pies in the residue. There had been more serious floods dating back when Rebecca was lady of the house.

Mum related an instance of her mother having to be rescued from rising waters. She had never graduated from water wings, either. The creek had risen so suddenly; it was above her head before she had a chance to vacate. Ever-resourceful Paddy came up with a somewhat intoxicated wife-evacuation plan.

A neighbour had a disused tin bath, which he and Paddy rendered watertight by securely fixing the plug. They then floated it over towards Rebecca waiting like an over-wept Juliet at the verandah rail. While the neighbour held the makeshift vessel steady, Paddy lifted his wife into the bath. This vessel was hardly Romeo material, however. An inappropriate movement from Rebecca caused it to tip sideways and dump her screeching and flailing into the water.

As the rain continued unabated over that June long-weekend in '67, it looked alarmingly like we were in for a repeat unceremonious-dunking (as with the original lady of the house, decades earlier). The washing machine had already been hoicked to higher ground beside the mango tree, then draped with a tarpaulin. Friends and neighbours strained to wobble the cumbersome piano over the side verandah. An army of music lovers paraded it up the hill, to the safety of Mr. & Mrs. C's under-house.

I felt a distinct prickle of apprehension when the water quickly rose above the highest level in my living memory. I hastily engaged in flood-level calculations, measuring how many gradients up my body before I panic-splashed out.

The search for altitude in the home was in full swing, as water began to seep inside. The furniture was raised apace. It felt like the last half of *A Night to Remember* (a black-and-white version of the Titanic story). All those who couldn't swim had abandoned ship to watch proceedings from a distance (only a few yards up the hill). The Grand House was one of the last in our lengthy street to be internally inundated. And still the rains came.

We spent the night at Mr. & Mrs. C's place. Overnight, we all woke at the same instant. The rain had stopped. We returned the next morning to survey the damage.

What greeted us was a yabby's dream home: all the slimy, stinking mire required to inspire the modern, discriminating crustacean to feel at one with his environment. To add further insult, a still worse chaos flowed in shortly after, when the rains started all over again.

The curious thing about the aftermath of this flood was the missing pieces; they went unnoticed for some considerable time. The eye grasps apprehensively for the immediate dreamtime items like the record collection and ballroom dresses. Only much later, while rummaging for a photo or memento, did anyone realise these no longer were.

When I was a child, I thought like a child and the underhouse was an Aladdin's Cave of the weird and wonderful. Aladdin must have gone in the '67 floods, too, because that was the last I saw of any of it. Gone to sea were the old Mawson ice-chest and the meat-safe. The air-raid warning-device was a wooden handle with a ratchet attached. If held above the head and swung like mad, it could render any living entity completely deaf within seconds. I never laid eyes on it again after the '67 floods.

Despite so much furniture upheaval and damage - a veritable Feng Shui crisis - our precarious financial position permitted replacement of bare essentials only. Unless it was totally beyond redemption (Bob Hope's last attempt at comedy springs to mind) it had to be returned to the living.

The plywood sections backing the bedroom suite, hand-carved by the Old Man decades earlier, soon rotted. Mum continued to store clothes inside. She was heavily into retro by this stage. I don't recall ever seeing Pat and Ted's classic rosewood hi-fi again. The version I purchased (after starting work) was retained as a storage box, once the internal workings had been dumped, along with the various tadpoles, baby crabs and a disoriented guppy.

For mum, flood losses paled to insignificance against the looming prospect of Royce's army service. After he embarked for a ten-week basic training at Singleton, she framed a photo of him looking dapper in fatigues. It was prominently displayed amongst the relentlessly lengthening gallery of familiar faces on the sideboard.

During those heart-stopping weeks, Royce phoned regularly to report his continuing existence. Mum got the impression he spent all his waking hours doing K.P. Obviously, whilst required to participate in the full spectrum of combat soldier-in-training activities, washing dishes and peeling spuds were duties he was least adept at skiving.

By the end of ten weeks, our favourite family Achilles' Heel - *Dodgy Back* - was forced out of the metaphorical closet by the rigours of military training.

Royce was released from compulsory service.

In hindsight, I think it more the pity armies of the world aren't composed entirely of soldiers of Royce's calibre. He doesn't have an aggressive bone in his body. This, coupled with the most laid-back attitude imaginable makes him a unique specimen in my unbiased opinion. He might have quoted the Redskin Peanut jingo verbatim but he would have had trouble remembering where he put that damn grenade four seconds ago.

By the time we celebrated Royce's twenty-first with a small party at The Grand House in January 1968, he was back in harness at the factory. This was where he had started as a fourteen-year old. With the trauma of a stint in the armed forces fading, Royce's thoughts returned to the recent floods. Before long, he resolved to build a boat, enabling occupants of The Grand House to be evacuated should a flood ever again reach such Biblical proportions.

I'll admit to being somewhat sceptical when he arrived home with plans in hand and some rudimentary materials to initiate this project. It seemed this *boat on the rebound* bizzo was likely to be a short romance. Yet, as he whistled, sawed and banged away under the house it became apparent he had closely observed the Old Man restore the big boat.

Scepticism turned to anticipation, from which sprang excitement as Royce reached the stage of painting on her name. He proudly called his vessel, Claudette, in honour of Little Claude's and Jen's beautiful new baby daughter. Royce invited family, neighbours and workmates to witness Claudette be officially launched near Federation Street. The Old Man was inconspicuous in his absence as the group assembled along the creek bank.

A few days earlier, the Old Man had presented his son with a small outboard motor. His rubicund face cheerfully glowed with pride for Royce's accomplishment. Royce broke a tall bottle of 4X over the bow, before pushing Claudette down the muddy bank to slop into the murky creek. At this juncture, it became apparent Royce's knowledge of boat building didn't extend to any practical water-related experience.

On reflection, his boat-wright's apprenticeship had been carried out on a clumsy old tug, which had never left the confines of the yard. I doubt if Royce could swim. (Neither of us ever made it to a single swimming lesson at Windsor State School.) As he struggled with starting the outboard, the undercurrent quickly carried the boat around the bend and out of sight of those waiting with bated breath on the creek bank.

Suddenly, back around the bend swam the Old Man, battling furiously against the tide. As he lurched from the water clad only in his baggy, white V-Fronts it was blatantly obvious to all and sundry that he was as full as a state school. That was hardly going to stop him rendering assistance to his son.

# Chapter Thirty Three

By 1969, Little Claude and Jen had been relocated to Darwin. Jen was expecting again, having given birth to Claudette whilst in Townsville. Ted had now struck out solo as a master builder. Various tasteful additions to the Paramount Estate at West Chermside testified to his craftsmanship. Patrice had been raised to factory supervisor, with a galley of male subordinates at her command. Royce was hanging onto the one and only job he ever held - excluding the nerve-shattering limbering up he received at Menzies' behest. I was the only working-age member of the family still capriciously tripping over one career path after another.

After twelve pleasurable months, I had moved effortlessly from junior filing-clerk to telephonist at Newstead. A couple of years down the track, a vacancy came up in the typing pool. Common sense dictated I knock back a secondary stenographer's position, considering shorthand was Greek to me. I had barely practiced it since being sacked for ineptitude from my first job, several years earlier. Yet, I was so grateful for the promotion, I foolishly accepted. Soon I was struggling to decipher the scribble on my notepad. At that point, the smart move would have been to brush up on shorthand during the weekends. Smart moves were never my forte. My over-riding instinct was simply to flee.

I perused the paper's job-sections for a fleeing position and applied for secretary to the Queensland manager of an insurance company. I'm *still* trying to work out the logic of that decision. Any rational thinker would have guessed the need for proficiency at shorthand in a private secretary's job. Whilst never having been held accountable for my left-brain activity, I did possess the luck of the Irish when it came to job interviews. This time was no different.

Suddenly, I was out of the quaint, predictable and sheltered typing pool of the suburbs and highflying it in a Queen Street green mirrorglass-and-steel tower. This Sydney-based company had just opened their Queensland branch. My immediate superior (the one and the same who interviewed me and subsequently offered me the job) and I were their only two employees in this state.

He was a conservative ex-banker, close to fifty years my senior.

That dear old codger had a day-long repertoire of exquisitely Dickensian work practices. He always carefully opened each item of mail along three sides, for close scrutiny. (You never knew if some cheque might be cunningly disguising itself as the dappled-blue interior of a standard-issue envelope.) He subsequently used the insides of those neatly unfolded missives as scribble paper for the remainder of the day.

I soon realised I had jumped in at the deep-end without my inflatables when the boss asked me to take notes for his forthcoming conference speech. A vivid premonition of combing through the employment pages came to me as he read through my typed draft. It was an impressionistic, vaguely abstract interpretation of his dictation. Fortunately, he recognised that *not* being a know-all is a healthy attitude for a beginner, so I avoided the humility of another sacking.

That was an isolated incident – thankfully! Shorthand was a minor part of the day's routine. When needs arose, my boss blew up the water-wings.

My core duties were processing insurance applications. Being from the old school, my boss calculated everything with pencil and paper. For my sake he purchased *a calculator* - I use the term loosely. The prototype was surely driven by a circle of slaves around a capstan. It functioned manually by winding a handle either forward or back depending whether you were multiplying or dividing. It would make a classy museum piece today if it has survived the ravages of time.

Once the bruises subsided after the stumbling phase in my new job, I bounded onwards and upwards. By the time I celebrated my nineteenth birthday, I was easily coping with a prestigious job at one of the better city addresses. My elevated work status came with all the associated trappings, including the latest IMB golf-ball typewriter. I was now looking down from my 16th floor window onto the very real-estate office I had left, tail between my legs, four years earlier.

If only the Ice Princess could see me now!

I made some drastic changes to my private life to fit the new image. After five years, I switched my patronage from Sandy Robertson's Dance Studio to the opposition Orchard's Dance Studio in Gipps Street, the Valley. Now I was on the amateur staff two nights a week. I trained for a couple of hours every Saturday morning with Peter, my new partner. Ballroom dancing is a great mover and shaper of teenage energy. Sadly, the unbelievably crass, backstabbing histrionics depicted in *Strictly Ballroom* are a naïve understatement of what really goes on.

# Chapter Thirty Four

The Paddy Fitzgerald of '69, as nature would have it, bore slight resemblance to the image evoked of a fit young sportsman decades earlier. The Pa I knew was old, bald and so bow-legged he seemed to be mounted on an invisible horse. The baldness arrived during his early twenties (I can't explain the horse). His everyday wardrobe was baggy khaki-trousers with a tight belt that had failed to locate the interiors of most loops. The belt was superfluous anyway, thanks to the braces he sported over the top of a grimy, white singlet. This princely undergarment was all too visible beneath a greying, unbuttoned shirt with sleeves rolled to the elbows.

Despite aching joints restricting his mobility - a legacy of his football days - he still remained active. In fact, he was hyperactive. Even to the point where he may have suffered from some obsessive-compulsive disorder, determining he devote the entire day to moving objects around the yard like pieces on a chessboard. He incessantly relocated mum's favourite pot-plants. When he tired of that, he would change up to the logs. He would secure rope to one end of a log, then haul it from backyard to front via the side lane, only to reverse the process later.

The atmosphere in the yard became positively frenetic.

Pa loved a roaring bonfire! This usually started with a sedate burning of old mango leaves raked up in the backyard. Then he became fixated with making it a festive occasion. He would throw anything and everything inflammable onto the heap. Generally, with a dipso's serendipity, he timed this outburst for when mum had a line full of clothes.

The pyromaniac gene recurred in Ella who adored a soaring backyard conflagration. After council regulations banned open fires, she could often be seen wearing black in public.

Pa's innovative grass-cutting techniques were worthy of note. Sometimes he used a reaping hook. However, the extreme pendulous action, coupled with a feverish grimace on his face frightened mum to the point of hiding the wretched thing. Undaunted, he would take to the grass with scissors (or anything with a blade at arm's length). I've even seen him with a Gem razorblade, holding each stem of grass up to make a clean slice.

He had the teeth-chattering habit of dropping any honed-steel blade exactly where he decided to call it quits. Any foot-lose and fancy-free frolicking after the event could end up learning the meaning of one of those nasty –ectomy words. The onset of crippling old age and the tireless shadowboxing of senility did nothing to curtail his lifelong pleasures - drinking and fighting. He was regularly banned from the Shamrock Hotel for starting brawls despite being 'well' into his seventies.

To give Pa his due, though, he confined his drinking to Saturdays (an act of temperance the Old Man never quite managed). Dan and Pa built up a good rapport - especially after Dan chose Rugby League as his preferred sport at Windsor State School. I imagine this is what re-ignited Pa's enthusiasm to pass on the secrets of the *Haka*, learned from his Kiwi friends while an international player.

Dan could always earn pocket money from his grandfather by running up to the nearest corner store. Pa would summons him from the side verandah and point to the Log Cabin tobacco tin on the duchesse. That was Dan's cue to shop for tobacco, paper and matches for which he was rewarded with a zack (sixpence). Our nearest corner store wasn't anywhere near a corner. It was behind the house. It had been there before Pa used to agist his horses in the adjoining paddock.

Operating a corner store used to be a respected and well-paid occupation. By '69, all that had changed. Their relegation to obscurity was in reverse proportion to the emergence of places like Brisbane Cash and Carry in the Valley. The opening of the first drive-in shopping centre in Australia in '59, opposite the Chermside tram terminus put another nail in the corner-store coffin.

When it was profitable to run a neighbourhood store attached to the family home, you could bet the owners had English or Irish surnames. A succession of immigrants extracted a lucrative living from the store out the back.

One such had two parrots in cages, ensuring customers were entertained whilst the shopkeeper weighed out spuds and wrapped them in newspaper. (The Health Department would have a fit today.)

As kids, we were forever running to the shop for mum's soda-water or Bex for Cecelia. By the time it came to Dan and Bart's turn to pop up the road for items overlooked at the supermarket, or Pa's smoking supplies, the owner had a Greek surname. He was barely managing to eke out a living for his family. If I'm not mistaken, Spiros would have been the last. That land, as well as the Oddfellows Hall next door were resumed for future road widening.

The road up the back was now a major artery. The ever-increasing volume of traffic, which had already claimed a fair share of victims from The Grand House was about to notch up another.

The Old Man had no-one to blame but himself, lurching off a tram in an intoxicated state straight into the path of an oncoming car. He landed unconscious in the gutter. An old chap who lived nearby witnessed the scene and was quick to call an ambulance.

By the time it arrived, the Old Man had regained consciousness, of sorts. It was obvious to everyone that he was paralytic. The ambulance officer declared him fit to go home. The big-hearted neighbour argued hospital was imperative. As it turned out, the Old Man underwent emergency surgery for multiple internal injuries including a broken pelvis. If he had come home he would have died of internal bleeding.

After awhile, he had improved enough to be sent over to Chermside Hospital for convalescence.

The artist then entered what became known as his Lamp Period. His therapy entailed constructing sundry bizarre lamps, using all colours of plastic tape carefully woven around a wire frame with an old bottle or something, as a base. Those lamps still turn up today in retro and secondhand shops. I recoil in horror whenever I spot one. The Old Man was always good at working with his hands, so he naturally excelled. The result was dozens of kitsch, psychedelic lamps cluttering the house (their utility being somewhat restricted by the lack of power points).

They did come in handy for engagements, birthdays or weddings when they could be simply dusted off and gift-wrapped.

# Chapter Thirty Five

By 1970, the tramlines had been pulled up and Dan was bussing it to Kedron High. Little Claude and Jen had been transferred to Brisbane. They bought with them their daughter, Claudette and new baby son, Sean-Claude. Little Claude's tales of his northern adventures, including being chased up a tree by a crocodile made Steve Irwin look like Barbara Cartland. His memoirs would certainly make a thrilling film. He lasted well in isolated places, such as Gove Peninsula and Groote Eyelandt. Jen became proficient at extracting giant frogs from the washing machine before loading the nappies.

While Jen was fighting her loosing battle with mould, Little Claude was struggling for a solution to his Aboriginal work-gangs disappearing on walkabout. I had the distinct feeling they had both fallen in love with the relaxed pace of northern Australia. Little Claude spoke with a faraway glint in his eyes about relaxing on the steps of the Darwin house, a finger over the top of his stubby while the rain turned into a waterfall.

On arriving in Brisbane, they stayed with Jen's parents at Doomben until they found a suitable rental over at Alderley. I loved that modern chamferboard cottage on the main drag just past the Alderley Arms Hotel. It was such a refreshing change from the pervasive dilapidation of The Grand House. I regularly made the trek down Newmarket Road for a visit.

As 1970 progressed, I was forced to consider my impending twenty-first birthday. The idea of a party was both appealing and appalling. The thought of my friends viewing living conditions at The Grand House so closely made me wince. Little Claude and Jen mercifully offered their home as a venue (pretty generous considering they had two tots).

Uncle Fergus's wife was easily persuaded into catering duties. Comforted by her culinary skills, I could at least depend on no great steaming botch-ups from that quarter. At the appropriate juncture (according to the Dorothy Bourke *Salon of Elegance: Rules of Etiquette*), I dispatched invitations to all and sundry, then anxiously waited (while balancing books on my head) for acceptances. The bulk was the crew from my dance studio plus obligatory relatives and otherwise-complaining neighbours.

I invited my boss and wife and they accepted with an enthusiasm that astonished me. Jen's mother worked in Tattersall's Club kitchens from which vantage she was able to ferret-out a punch recipe with a difference. It involved assorted citrus juices and a catering-sized bottle of gin. Royce had won the social-club raffle at work a week before the party. The prize was such an enormous bottle of Ballantyne's Scotch, it came with its own tilting stand.

My friends being generally moderate drinkers, the Scotch was secreted to a bedroom with Uncle Fergus in charge of distribution. I knew the punch was a winner as soon as one die-hard beerophile appeared to have been hypnotised by the punchbowl. When word got out about the Scotch in a bedroom, a swathe was cut through the hallway lingerers. Uncle Fergus always was a pushover.

The night was an overwhelming success (if I do say so myself). I didn't quite catch the story of how the Old Man ended up dunked headfirst into the rubbish-bin filled with ice for soft drinks. No-one was game to touch his false teeth the next day, when they were discovered perched on the gatepost beside the bin in question. Patrice drove him back over to Little Claude's, once he had sobered, so he could retrieve the offending item himself.

Naturally my cousin, Little Fergus had been invited. I was staggered when he introduced his date as *my fiancée*. He was two years my junior. He appeared enthralled with her all night. This left me with confused emotions. Naturally, I was pleased to see him so happy. But the green-eyed monster raised its ugly head. I wasn't jealous of *him* but of his partnering skills: I hadn't managed to snare a big knight for my big night. If only the others had stayed single, my solo status wouldn't have grated so painfully.

Within a few months of the party, Little Fergus's engagement was off. His ex-fiancée moved back to New Zealand. That was probably the catalyst for his enduring tendency to drown in brown anaesthetic.

Alcohol affects people so individually: take my eldest cousin, for example. He made the newspapers one time he performed a rain-dance, naked on the bar at the Breakfast Creek Hotel. I feel sure the standard of the impromptu performance would have been artistically relevant and couldn't be dismissed simply as some depraved dipso's mindless exhibitionism. Our Irish heritage endowed us with an innate

116

appreciation for rhythm. And I'm entirely confident rain would have fallen the very next day (somewhere in the world).

By '71, Little Claude and Jen had scraped up a deposit for their own home. They chose a cute bungalow walking distance to her parents at Doomben. One of life's little synchronicities had occurred: that house was next door to the Aboriginal lady's grandson. She once lived on Stratton Street, next to Little Claude's paternal grandfather. By now, those Stratton Street residences had been replaced by commercial and industrial properties.

Life, like a beautifully crafted metronome, paced out a tidy rhythm for Patrice and Ted. They had purchased a block in the burgeoning new suburb of Aspley. Now they excitedly discussed plans for that dream-home Ted was soon to build.

Around this time, Bart introduced Basil.

Basil was an Alsatian who supposedly followed Bart home from school. I have a strong suspicion a trail of chocolate-chip cookies came into play. Regardless, Basil stayed on to replace Horse as the cherished mongrel of The Grand House.

# Chapter Thirty Six

After a succession of instructors had been driven round the bend, Royce managed to pass his test. He purchased a splendid white, pushbutton Valiant, from a car dealer on the south side who happened to be a prominent trotting identity. It was unanimous at The Grand House: his car was so damn stylish, it could be hired out for weddings.

Royce remained a betting man, although his interest in horsepower had shifted down a gear, from gallopers to trotters. His Valiant wheels were bound to reach Border Park, at Tweed Heads, for their night meetings.

That Royce's laid-back attitude had become a distinctive hallmark of his identity was etched on all our minds, one return trip from Border Park.

Royce was with Karl, trundling north along the Pacific Highway from the trots. There came a loud buzzing, which continued unabated for several klicks until the car and the buzz stopped, simultaneously. Royce then observed a red light flashing on the dashboard and steam hissing from the engine. He fumbled around in the dark to open the bonnet (a first, for him). Even to someone not in the least mechanically minded, like Royce, the radiator being out of water must have been about as ambiguous as tabloid headlines. He scratched his prematurely balding head.

'No-one told me I had to *keep on* putting water into it!' he muttered.

So he hoofed it up the bleak night highway. Eventually, he came across a vintage servo with a motel out the back, all closed up for the evening. Nevertheless, after foraging he found an empty tin, which he filled with water for the dehydrated Valiant. It was a tedious marathon getting home that night and an expensive lesson for Royce.

He just shrugged it off. Upsetting Royce would be a thankless chore, to be sure. It was his innate equanimity that enabled him to work at the same tedious job day in day out, despite several changes in factory ownership and location.

Observing Royce's car-struck freedom, since he graduated from pedestrian; I determined to venture onto wheels. There was first the hurdle of a driving licence to be knocked over. It seemed to take an inordinate amount of time and money before my instructor was game enough to book me in for the test.

Having truly earned my licence, I set eyes on a faded pink-and-grey Triumph Herald parked outside the Strathpine Country Club with $150 scrawled across the windscreen. I saw my destiny. As a precaution, I asked Royce along for advice on matters mechanical. (His expertise with radiators was invaluable.)

Once a done deal, he and Karl followed behind as I drove my sporty compact back to The Grand House. Karl had access to spray-painting equipment from his line of work at the factory. Within a couple of weeks, we had transformed the bleached out pink and grey job into a mustard and black motoring masterpiece.

My compact, *almost* sports car and I became inseparable. Despite three tram-services running virtually through our backyard, I drove the short distance to my job in the city. Image is everything. (It was no longer cool to be seen on public transport.)

The world of drive-in shopping centres was opened up to mum on Saturday mornings. No more lugging dilly-bags home from the Valley.

It wasn't long before I ventured as far as Surfer's Paradise. I'll never forget that combined feeling of exhilaration and apprehension as *I* drove off down the Pacific Highway. A brave new world was opening up to me.

A couple of girlfriends and I experienced the sheer delight of having our own cheap, yet comfortable pad for an entire week of freedom from families. Freedom came at the idyllically positioned *Crumby Bum* Hotel (as the in-crowd call it). Nestled into the side of Currumbin Hill, back-lit by sapphire blue Pacific Ocean: it won our Best Spot award for the Gold Coast, summer of '71. We screamed and cheered away the afternoons as Sounds Incorporated belted out cover-versions of our raviest bee-bop shang-a-lang pop tunes.

Evenings, we would promenade to the Pink Elephant Bar at the Chevron Hotel, pretending to infiltrate *the aristocracy* of so lordly priced an establishment. (We already argued the toss earlier in the day, deciding who got the single bed in our considerably less ritzy lodgings down the street). We hadn't heard of lesbians at that stage; so sharing a double bed wasn't the occasion for screamingly self-conscious carry-ons.

Party spirits took a nosedive when, just after that holiday Nanny died in hospital at Chermside. It was February '72. Her death wasn't unexpected. She had ailed a long while.

Disorientation then set in and we all went into a state of shock when, only weeks later, mum found Pa lifeless in bed. Paddy died on St Patrick's Day. (Now, *that's* synchronicity.) In the short space of three weeks we buried Nanny at Toowong next to her husband, Frederick and Pa, at Lutwyche, next to Rebecca.

After that sombre start to the year, the residents of The Grand House *unanimously* resolved to give mum a break. She hadn't sampled anything remotely resembling a holiday since the unforgettable camping trip to Wellington Point. That was another lifetime ago, when Royce was still in nappies and Dan and I were just a ruddy glimmer in the Old Man's bloodshot eye. The nine of us reaching a unanimous decision on anything was a first in itself. And second most flabbergasting was everyone agreeing to *my* suggestion of renting the flat I spotted, on the main highway at Surfer's (the preceding Christmas break).

One quick phone-call and it was booked for Easter.

Mum was genuinely thrilled at the prospect of a holiday. Patrice and Ted were happy to remain in the emptier home and baby-sit assorted cats and Charlie (a white, sulphur-crested cockatoo Royce brought home years ago). Charlie never thanked anyone for its captivity and at every opportunity shattered the air with its cantankerous liberationist hullabaloo.

As the Easter weekend approached, one of the worst cyclones in living memory crossed the coast further north, wreaking havoc on the Whitsunday Islands. The residual effects of Ada soon blew down to southeast Queensland. The rain set in as we arrived at our quarters.

Despite the joke weather, mum thoroughly enjoyed the sheer aimlessness of a sojourn at a sopping beach resort.

When Easter Monday dawned, it was still bucketing down; we decided to hit the road early to avoid the traffic. Up till this point, I hadn't challenged the Triumph with anything of such pelting magnitude. Wending our way back along the highway towards Brisbane, Dan and I were closely followed by Karl and Royce ferrying the remainder of the holidaymakers.

The wind and rain recklessly buffeted our low-slung dinghy. Every time we splashed through a puddle, it would spray up through the floor causing the motor to cough and splutter (my nerves going off like sparklers). By the time we reached The Grand House, we couldn't have become more drenched if we had gone to the Underwater Masquerade Ball disguised as sponges.

As the sun shone brilliantly next weekend, Royce and Karl filled the Triumph with a product un-retentively called *bog*. Eventually, so much of the car was replaced by bog, I thought of it as a terracotta model - something that could turn to chalk-dust in an accident. I nursed Triumph of Bog along for another year or so, until I could afford something less friable.

Oddly enough, when the time came to upgrade, I could find no-one remotely interested in taking Bog off my hands. She was parked in the backyard, on hallowed Model-T ground. Before dust returned to dust, she became useful for Dan to practice the basics of driving.

# Chapter Thirty Seven

After more than ten years on the trot, or foxtrot, I canned the dancing shoes. I figured it was time to catch up on the education I sidestepped with dodging, diving, ducking and weaving strategies that would have made the Olympic netball team look like rhinos on rollerblades.

Not long afterwards, with my usual flair for jumping first and expiating later, I scoffed at the job security I had built up in insurance over four years. The desire to return to real estate was just a whim. Many a time down the track, I have pondered the wisdom of such a cavalier attitude toward my old boss - when he phoned and asked me to return. (My replacement must have been having trouble coming to grips with the steam-driven calculator.)

In '73, Dan was entering year eleven at Kedron High with an enthusiasm to learn (an impetus that entirely eluded me at his age). Bart and Dan were both seriously involved with Rugby League. Bart was enrolled with the under-13s in the famous Fortitude Valley Rugby League Football Club (commonly known as 'Valleys' and affectionately as 'The Diehards'). Bart trained and played at Emerson Park, at Stafford. Home turf for the seniors was Neuman Oval, at Albion.

Dan was part of Kedron High's successful team. Kedron was once a force to be reckoned with on the Rugby League playing field. Photos of various triumphant school-teams used proudly to adorn Kedron Park Hotel's private bar. Fortitude Valley Rugby League Football Club was arguably Brisbane's finest in that era. They picked up many of Kedron High's more gifted players.

Everyone at The Grand House was a rabid Diehards' supporter and fellow followers were everywhere. Happy Jack was a particularly unforgettable inclusion. His eccentric behaviour gave me the impression he definitely lived too long *in sniff* of Newstead's gasometers.

During any game in progress, he ran relentlessly around the perimeter of the oval. Whilst engaged in this feverish activity, he delivered inane instructions to all and sundry on field. Invariably, altercations with supporters of the opposing team would flare. Happy Jack was such a popular personality, he was never charged admission to a Neuman Oval match. I also believe he never had to jiggle his pockets for the cost of a drink at the club bar.

We regularly attended home games at Neuman Oval and never missed a final at Lang Park. Our family's affinity with the Diehards could be traced to Stratton Street. By coincidence, the father of an erstwhile key player was the bloke whose wife would hurl him downstairs when he got home pissed after the Waterloo. If our beloved Diehards were in the grand final, Royce's car would be festooned with white-and-blue ribbons. He would then take 'the scenic route' to Lang Park - via the opposition's home turf.

Royce still cringes about the day we drove back across the Hornibrook Highway, after a *Cook's Tour* of enemy territory, Redcliffe. Mum entertained herself by bellowing abuse through the backseat window to Redcliffe supporters, while poor red-faced Royce, in the driver's seat wilted with embarrassment and the prospect of retaliation.

Grand finals at Lang Park could only be described as breathtaking, even if the weather wasn't always conducive. One year it rained so heavily, Paul Hogan, alias The Winfield Man, looked like he had melted into a liquid dinner-suit after one circuit in the sports car. He received scant attention however, as the cheerleaders wet costumes clung so transparently to their pert parts, the boys in the outer were wiping drool off their chins.

One spectator became so excited he tore off his clothes and streaked across the field. With the thin blue line in hot pursuit, he led them on a merry chase ducking in and out of proceedings on the oval. They finally had to tackle him to bring him down. He was escorted from the ground to a rousing applause.

Whilst Bart enjoyed Sunday afternoons at the football with us; Ted's Sundays went into finishing the palace he had built for his family at Aspley. In its construction phase, likely bets from drinkers at the nearby Aspley Hotel would have been odds-on for a church more than a residence, the roofline being so eccentrically lofty. It was a massive home with four bedrooms, two bathrooms, office, sunken lounge with fireplace and a double lockup garage.

Ted had certainly come a long way from the orphanage.

# Thirty Eight

1974 started in traditional style for the occupants of The Grand House, groaning to recover from Christmas hedonism. This time, an English couple who occupied the duplex next door joined us. It wasn't our first shared Christmas lunch. Mr. and Mrs. Wood were on their second tenure in the flats. They had lived in the front duplex, years before returning to the Old Dart.

They were a lovely old couple who could never make up their minds which country felt like heartland. They embraced the extraordinary customs of native Brisbanites, yet couldn't resist the pull of those antiquated Tudor villages nestled into emerald green hills and the BBC. Consequently, they repeatedly crossed the oceans of half the globe, grudging nomads between two antipodean islands.

They did, however, sometimes flounder with the intricacies of social protocol. Mrs. Wood tells of a party invitation, to which everyone was asked to *bring a plate*. It seemed highly enigmatic. Being keen to ingratiate herself, she transported her entire dinner set to ensure there were no shortages.

Little Claude and Ted also developed fascinating anomalies that Christmas. The pair regularly became obsessed with inventing ornate and bizarre schemes to set themselves up and be financially secure for life. So, nobody took much notice the afternoon they lurked around the old washtubs, which they had filled with water. I recall overhearing a comment along the lines of:

'If the Arabs find out what we're up to, we're dead meat!'

It appears they had figured a way to propel a motor, using the energy with which a ping-pong ball rises, after being pushed to the bottom of a quantity of water. The sole remaining problem was transferring the theory from the washtub to the road. I could understand Little Claude hatching this kind of madness. After all, he was partial to a drink and sometimes played *being silly*. But I don't know what Ted's excuse was. He was virtually teetotal.

Mum's new-year agenda began with equipping Dan for his senior year at Kedron. One of her children was at last making it through high school non-stop. She was glowing with pride for her youngest son. Having purchased the stipulated items, she placed them carefully in a bundle on top of the wardrobe in the sleep-out, blissfully unaware of its journey ahead.

The Australia Day long-weekend of '74 saw the worst flooding in Brisbane this century. The '67 experience served as a painful reminder that The Grand House was smack in the middle of a flood plain. As the rains continued unabated, Royce and Dan began the nervous ritual of checking the creek at the end of the street. How fast was the current running? Were the stormwater drains coping?

Their regular reconnaissance throughout the day brought no assurance. The relentless hammering rain on the tin roof ensured meagre sleep as we lay in bed that night. The full moon, occasionally visible between pitch clouds, threatened a king tide.

Mercifully, daybreak brought a break in the weather. As the longed-for sun appeared in a radiant blue sky, flood warnings blared incessantly over the transistor. We didn't need to be told! In the stark light of day, we could see the creek had broken its banks and was rapidly encroaching.

There was a general frenzy of semi-organized chaos. Barely in time did the washing machine and lawnmower get to higher ground - beyond the broken-down back fence adjoining the derelict Oddfellows Hall.

Already the now *two* screeching cockatoos, their cages kept at the bottom of the backstairs, were delivering a deafening version of their usual cacophony. Their hasty re-positioning to the dining room only added to the pandemonium inside. They danced and screeched with abandon as mum furiously packed up linen and other odds and sods.

Fortunately, Ted and Patrice's almost completed house at Aspley provided a safe haven. Time and tide waits for no man. Cecelia had been evacuated to Little Claude and Jen's house the previous day. (There was no space left on the eardrum for her hysterics in this frenzy.) Basil, the dog, wasn't sure what was awry, so he took to diving off the front verandah swimming down the side lane then in through the backdoor. At this point, he shook over everyone and every thing, before taking off on another round trip.

A distress call from the duplex next door prompted the launch of Claudette, the mighty mini-ark. Royce ferried a grateful Mr. & Mrs. Wood, clutching meagre possessions, to the safety of dry land. Their jovial reception of these events was inspirational. Having lived through the Blitz and years of food rationing, this was probably a barrel of laughs. They may have privately cursed the timing of this current sojourn in their home away from home from home.

Royce's little rowboat had its work cut out that morning. Flooding was so widespread across Brisbane, the SES had no chance. It was left to neighbours to help each other with anything that floated. Those living closer to the creek were soon on their rooftops awaiting rescue.

Though most were complete strangers, suddenly there were no barriers between people.

A small flotilla of crafts, including Claudette went about busily plucking people, pets and prized possessions from the rapidly rising waters. My phobia of water saw me beat a hasty retreat to watch events unfold from a much higher vantage. I sat inside my car, which had been relocated the previous day. It felt as though I were watching a bizarre Sensurround matinée at the drive-in. The scenes unfolding contained all the elements of a blockbuster disaster movie -- pathos, perplexity, heroics and humour.

Rescue craft deposited evacuees as close to dry land as possible. Most looked stunned, wading through the shallows, clutching a baby, a purse, a box or a bag. With nowhere else to go, many then simply gazed in disbelief at the murky, garbage-strewn inland-sea, dotted with oblong islands of tin, fibro and tile roofs.

The grandson of Pa's old adversary, the Masonic Lodge member walked to the top of his stairs to assess the situation. A few minutes later he returned decked in bright yellow board-shorts, a surfboard under arm. He launched the board, threw himself on top then paddled up and down the street.

Once the water began pouring into the lowest corner of The Grand House, those who hadn't already done so saw it as their cue to vacate. The cockatoos in their respective cages were loaded in Claudette, screeching raucously while being rowed by an increasingly hearing-challenged person to the higher ground of Mr. & Mrs. C.'s place. The water was rising at such an horrific pace, there wasn't time to shift the piano, before scrambling to safety to play the waiting game.

Waiting at a dry remove further up the street, mum suddenly remembered Dan's school requisites on the wardrobe. Ted and Little Claude hurried to the rescue. They rowed back to tear a section off the roof, which they calculated to be above the wardrobe. Like a couple of SAS troopers they pinpointed, reached in and rescued the package from the rising water.

What followed was a long night. Royce, Dan and Karl sat in the latter's Valiant Regal parked outside Mr. & Mrs. C's. There was little shut-eye for anyone due to one cockatoo perpetually crying, 'Royce!' whereupon the other would screech, 'Shut Up!'

That was the worst flood in living memory. Although we lost virtually everything, we weren't on our Pat Malone. We had to dump the piano and *His & Hers* bedroom suite. It was all beyond redemption. I felt an eerie hesitancy, first stepping inside The Grand House to be confronted with so many displaced objects covered in mud.

A gallery of black-and-white faces looked on from the dining-room walls.

# Chapter Thirty Nine

The floods weren't the last tempest of '74. Mum's health had been less than promising - hardly surprising after all the stress she had suffered. Stress always seems remediable, sometime in the future until the news of cancer finds everyone sleeping in security. The prompt and accurate diagnosis of the disease in her kidney region was, in no small way, attributable to the diligence of a local Indian doctor.

Check-ups with the neighbourhood medic were a luxury our family purse could never stretch to while we were growing up. Before Medicare, the ten-and-six outlay was well beyond our resources. It would be the public hospital's casualty before accidents or illnesses were diagnosed.

Our closest GP - when I was young enough to be careless about youth - worked out of a surgery behind a high fence overgrown with lantana. Considering the Old Man only ever referred to him as The Butcher, I was only too thrilled never to have to see him.

Mum had a ready pharmacopoeia for most minor ailments and injuries. A Reckitts blue bag would take the pain out of bee stings, whilst a gold band rubbed across an emerging sty promptly clears it from the eye. For his part, the Old Man reckoned a tablespoon of castor oil would cure every conceivable internal ailment. The enthusiasm with which he applied Vick's chest rub looked like the onset of *grand mal.*

By '74, the lantana-covered surgery had been replaced by a servo. It was suddenly within everyone's financial reach to consult a local doctor who, fortunately for us, happened to be this Indian at Rosemount.

Despite the vested interest in denouncing our public-health system, I argue we have at least jumped one big rung up the evolutionary ladder, compared to countries like the U.S. where everything serves the rich, and that's it. The fact that some public facilities are archaic doesn't mean we would be better off without them. The standard of compassionate care is exemplary. Emergency treatment *should* be dispensed on a priority basis, morally speaking, with no regard as to whether a critical patient can afford to be rescued.

With minimal delay, mum was put under the surgeon's knife at the Royal Brisbane Hospital to have a cancer-ridden kidney removed.

Unfortunately, the local doctor's prognosis for the Old Man was unlikely to be fixed by a surgeon's knife. Years of overdosing on alcohol had atrophied his brain cells. Although he no longer indulged, the condition was irreversible. He was away in never-never land most of the time. Perhaps it was the same never-never land the alcohol used to take him to. He tended to maunder around the streets, perhaps with less of a zigzag than when sloshed, but no less aimlessly.

On the evening of mum's surgery, he wandered off, again! On this occasion, it was raining like a tidal wave curling out of the sky. Knowing the first question on mum's lips would be, *How's your father?* we drove around looking for him before the visit. As soon as we spotted Basil in the Valley, we knew the Old Man wouldn't be far away. That noble hound had a sixth sense about the watchful eye this old bloke needed. Basil mooched along after him whenever he traipsed off.

Mum's recovery was variable, on the side of troublesome and hindered by anxieties for her husband (who was in and out of hospital on a regular basis). I was always agog at her unquestioning devotion to the Old Man. Whenever he was hospitalised, she would be there spoon-feeding him daily. Eventually, because they didn't know where to pigeonhole his condition, he ended up in Ward 16.

There he remained for a few weeks.

One day, on one of mum's bedside feeding visits, the nurse on duty brought her up to date. Because they could do nothing to reverse his condition, he was to be transferred to the mental facility at Goodna.

That news struck a dissonant chord with her. She immediately arranged his release from Ward 16.

For what seemed an interminable period after that, he was in and out of hospital. Eventually, a bed became available at Mount Olivett Hospice.

The year was 1977.

# Chapter Forty

After the '74 floods, Mr. and Mrs. Wood in the duplex next to The Grand House decided to move back to England. The thought of moving to sunny England to get away from the rain in Australia I found quite piquant. That meant they no longer needed their bubble Morris car. Dan had been driving the old Triumph around the backyard for months, just hanging out to be old enough to take his test. When the big day came, we jumped at the opportunity to buy the Morris, going for the not so princely sum of fifty bucks. Dan was king of the road, *driving* to Kedron High every day for the rest of his senior year.

After that last flood, Ted, Patrice and Bart never lived at The Grand House again. They became uncritically besotted with their Aspley mansion. Bart chose to stay on at Kedron High, as opposed to the nearer school at Aspley. Dan gave him a lift home to The Grand House each afternoon. They hung around together with Dearie, until one of his parents collected him after work. Patrice's factory had been relocated to Geebung. Ted's work could be almost anywhere, relative to the house he was constructing at the time.

After the Triumph Herald, I moved temporarily to a Vauxhall Viva. It was a sister to the one Little Claude and Jen had purchased to hit the newlywed road. I mention this in passing because I put it in for its first service and it fell off the hoist! That little *Whoops!* saw me once more in the market for secondhand wheels.

After scouring the classifieds one Saturday morning, I and my auto-centric entourage, which included Royce, Karl and Dan explored all the way to Cleveland. As the bayside breezes blew, we found ourselves scrutinising what lay under the bonnet of an ex cop-car. It looked a likely candidate, albeit with a price tag higher than a hippie on the third day of a rock festival. By now, it was dawning on me that Royce's mechanical expertise might not quite match his confidence.

Dan, on the other hand, was learning about motors the fast way, through practical experience. He was still a bit too young, however, to have any managerial say in such critical decisions. In this delicate predicament, we asked the vendor if we could test-drive the Falcon over to Ted's place so he could share his expertise.

Ted gave the vehicle a thorough inspection then, without the least trace of a flinch, he wrote a cheque out for the full amount!

I was simply staggered at this unexpected and unsolicited act of generosity. I sheepishly handed over my wad of notes (several hundred below the cheque). He calmly suggested I pay him the rest, whenever. It took only a month or so to settle the debt but a lifetime won't dim the memory of his big-heartedness.

Kind gestures, unlike diamonds, are forever.

Later that same year, Dan passed his senior exams. Almost immediately he became a Trainee Manager with *Top* Woolworths, in the Valley. His elevated station demanded a cooler image. The Morris just *had* to go! A '68 gold Falcon sedan, with more lights than a Gold Coast Christmas Tree took its place. He was quickly promoted through the ranks, starting with fruit-and-veg manager, then up to merchandising manager. From there, he moved to their prestigious Queen Street store. He subsequently scaled the dizzy heights to an executive position at Toowoomba.

His relocation to Toowoomba didn't please mum one iota. Dan would swan home regularly in his latest, no less than a Ford LTD. The vehicle was undeniably luxurious, if a tad past its prime. The last time I saw it was at the foot of the Toowoomba Ranges with the bonnet raised. He then opted for a more reliable, if less imposing, Ford. This lasted until he was promoted to assistant manager at Burleigh Heads. That posting was possibly the highpoint of his career. What more could a bloke, barely in his twenties, ask? He had his own little fibro pad at Staghorn Avenue, Surfer's Paradise and an executive position in the retail industry.

Whilst Dan was clawing his way up the corporate ladder in retail, my step backwards into real estate proved not the wisest move ever made. The housing sector was in a slump, prospects looked gloomy.

Despite now having a senior certificate and a couple of tertiary units in real-estate law and valuation, the good old days of ample job opportunities were already a wistful memory. I was struggling to meet the repayments on yet another vehicle trade up.

I finally snared a husband in June '77. Anthony (who is not Roman) and I were married in the Registry Office downstairs in the Old Treasury Building. I have a feeling mum breathed a private sigh of relief. (I may have been proving even more wayward than my siblings.)

In October that same year, the Old Man finally called it a day at Mount Olivett.

Dan was working at Woolworths in the Valley that particular Saturday morning. Someone asked his boss to pass on the news. His superior gave Dan permission to leave early. Dan declined the offer without any visible sign of emotion, then resumed the task at hand.

For my part, I hadn't been near the Old Man since he was admitted to Mount Terminal.

It was many years down the track before I could wring some equanimity out of the whole experience. Looking back, I can better understand alcoholism as the mental health issue it is. The need to escape on a permanent basis with any kind of drug suggests profound dissatisfactions that are only ever treated symptomatically. The Old Man was buried at Lutwyche Cemetery not far from his son, Russell.

Ted insisted he wanted to meet the funeral expenses of someone who had welcomed him into his home, when he was a lost and lonely teenager.

Such are the hearts of the loneliest hunters.

# Chapter Forty One

In August '78, mum went onto the aged pension. This afforded her the first secure, albeit desperately modest income since retiring at twenty from Dalgety's. A lot of water had inundated the old flood plain in the interim. Now her eldest grandson, Bart had completed his senior year and was working as a labourer for his father. Whilst Ted continued to build impressive homes, he had formulated a mid-life crisis plan, when he figured he would lack the stamina to tackle such demanding work. He acquired a parcel of land on the northern outskirts of Brisbane, in an area that used to be dairy farms. The zoning allowed for the operation of a wrecking yard.

Going way back to the days when he and Little Claude tinkered with their stockcar Saturday afternoons, Ted had ever since enjoyed tipping himself under the bonnet of a car. This is now where he saw his future.

Whilst Dan had virtually walked from the school gate into his position at Woolworths, there had been little let up in the increasing demands of climbing the corporate ladder. Lack of flexibility with holidays and so many unpaid, workaholic hours along the way were taking their toll. During an office relocation he injured his back and, since then, suffered spasmodic excruciating pain.

I'm not sure whether it was because future advancement would be dependent on his relocation to Melbourne, or whether it was simply a case of burnout. Towards the end of '79, Dan resigned. At the time, he was managing a suburban store.

1979 was significant for me with the arrival of my son, Benjamin.

In 1980, Ted and Bart constructed a simple brick shed on the land at Pine Rivers. Ted then purchased an old Bedford tow-truck in order to accumulate stock. This was the humble beginning of the wrecking yard. Before long, trade was brisk enough to demand the services of an extra. The obvious choice was Dan who, to date, hadn't found permanent employment following his abrupt exit from the retail industry.

Ted's elder brother, Bill, who recently retired from the wharf, would call at the wrecking yard on a daily basis. The pair sat and yarned for hours, speculating on world-shattering issues like the day when the road outside would become a four-lane highway.

By now, Patrice had been working for twenty years at a job she once started purely out of financial desperation. That was when Bart was a baby. She since became head honcho on the factory floor in charge of a large, predominantly male staff. It was both physically and emotionally exhausting, voraciously consuming the best years of her life.

It took no extraordinary feat of persuasion, then, once Ted recommended she put her feet up. Putting her feet up was just what she had in mind, but not the way Ted imagined. Immediately on retiring, she took to aerobics, jazz-ballet and tap-dancing with an enthusiasm that beggared all belief.

By 1980, Royce hadn't missed a beat in the job he started at fourteen. He was now in his thirties. While the job specification barely altered from one year to the next, the working environment had been given a facelift with a new lady boss on the factory floor.

Roslyn was a human dynamo who thrived on keeping machines ticking over. She wasn't averse to giving anyone - be they the toughest of blokes - a verbal kick in the 'nads to achieve that end.

In the embryonic stages of their friendship, Roslyn was embroiled in a terrifying relationship with a fellow prone to violence. This could have been the reason she felt drawn to Royce's gentle nature. Having rashly gone public on their mutual interest, they were immediately confronted with hostility on two sides.

The miffed ex-boyfriend proved to be the easier of the two. A phone call from Little Claude, posing as a fortune-teller did the trick. (Little Claude can sound quite convincingly portentous when needs be.)

On the other hand, mum's cool attitude towards Roslyn only served to drive a wedge between her and her son, one that prevented amiability for many years.

Turning their backs to the cool wind from The Grand House, Royce and Roslyn searched elsewhere to set up home. Pretty soon, Kojak joined them. Kojak was a foal Royce agisted in a paddock not far from where he and Roslyn eventually landed.

He finally had his horse.

# Chapter Forty Two

By 1980, it was stark staringly obvious The Grand House needed renovating. My conscience was clawing and nagging me about it. My new family was ensconced in a comfortable, comparatively lavish rental while mum continued to live in almost third-world conditions. Siblings who had so far flown the coup, now enjoyed twentieth-century amenities. This was something none of us could deprive her of much longer.

A memory photo: I took my new baby over to The Grand House for the first time. As he lay sleeping on the bed I once slept in, those few years before I outwardly bounded, mum looked down adoringly at him. She wistfully deliberated whether she would live to see him celebrate his twenty-first. Although she was only sixty-one, she was truly battle-wearied.

As poor as her health was, she fared better than Cecelia whose crippling arthritis had been compounded, years after her retirement, with peptic ulcers and deteriorating kidney function. If these two dear doddery old darlings were to have any quality in their remaining lives under that Swiss-cheese roof then, at the very least, the bathroom and toilet would have to be relocated upstairs.

It didn't take a Rhodes Scholar to appreciate the minimum outlay was going to be a maximum wallop and well beyond a couple of pensioners. One hot-potato idea being tossed about was to raise a loan against the property. What with its tumbledown condition, coupled with the land having been severely inundated in '74, I doubted many lending institutions would see it as collateral for anything more than a few delightful shells.

Before any action could be taken, the smoggy topic of The Grand House's ownership needed to be clarified. My life-study class taught me, if there are pickings to be had, vultures circle well before the corpse is cold. Bearing in mind a property was involved: it seemed extraordinary there had been no mention of a will since Paddy's demise. Mum was all but confident the house had been bequeathed to Fergus, Cecelia and her, in equal shares. That confidence was somewhat tenuously founded on her brief sighting of a document many years earlier, while relocating Pa in readiness for Ted's arrival.

Since her father's death, she had let it all go to seed. She was undoubtedly terrified at the prospect of the house being sold into a three-way split. This was the only home she ever knew. Notwithstanding its ramshackle condition, those earliest memories were in grain. And that creates a sturdy resilience to faddy mod cons.

I could also understand why Cecelia hadn't bothered pursuing the will. How far could she expect to go on one-third share, even if she weren't heavily reliant on her sister as a carer? Uncle Fergus was the only one who would benefit from a division. His restraint in money-up-for-grabs circumstances was commendable, even curious.

The situation had now reached critical point. It no longer mattered why nothing had been done. It was just imperative that repairs preempted the place being condemned.

My siblings and I reached a loose consensus (as opposed to a unanimous decision) on a plan of action. It more or less entailed mum and Cecelia handing over their share of the property, in exchange for lifelong occupancy of the renovated house. This left just Uncle Fergus's share to be financed over and above the cost of improvements.

Armed with that idea, we set off to see Uncle Fergus.

We were oblivious to the fact that, as sure as mum had been the estate was divided in three, Uncle Fergus was equally convinced it had been bequeathed solely to him. That devious old bastard Paddy Fitzgerarld had told him as much on several occasions.

That confrontation with Uncle Fergus set the cat amongst the pigeons. Certainly those in Anzac Square sprang to the sky for their lives as the parties concerned dashed to the Public Trustee Office, located just off the square. By the time the last bird had settled, it turned out mum was right. Nevertheless, the familiar banter had become somewhat splintered. The pigeons strutted cautiously about, darting nervous glances as the party re-crossed the square.

That hurdle having been knocked over without too many broken legs, the next was to establish a fair market-value for the place in its existing state. Then we would estimate the cost of rendering it habitable. It came down to the fact that we were all going to have to turn our pockets inside out.

Little Claude, having just collaborated in a business partnership was well and truly strapped for cash. Even despite the cool climate continuing between Royce's partner Roslyn and mum, they didn't have that sort of money. Dan was struggling to get back on his feet after

136

months out of work. Tony and I were supporting four children - another story in itself.

Patrice was uniquely capable of raising the considerable funds. She had recently received a retirement payoff for twenty years' service. Ted nobly considered the money hers exclusively, to do with as she wished.

So it was, fifty-five years after Paddy first financed construction of The Grand House, it passed directly into the hands of his first-born grandchild.

Patrice was as good as her word. Under Ted's watchful eye, the old place was knocked back into shape again. The original outer shell was concealed under that artificial chamferboard product, which Telemarketers flog to death. The leaky tin roof was covered with imitation tiles. The place had to be re-levelled, replacing the rotting wooden-stumps with concrete ones. New fences went up all around; concrete was poured down the side lane and throughout the under-house. Finally, a brand-new bathroom and toilet were installed upstairs, adjacent to a lovely little patio where mum and Cecelia could relax and enjoy the morning sun.

The only discernable remnants of The Grand House, circa 1925, was the single Queen Victoria rose bush in a corner of the front yard and the mango tree dominating the back.

The first houseguest would have been pleased about that.

# Chapter Forty Three

The business partnership Little Claude so enthusiastically embarked upon had, within a relatively short time, ended acrimoniously. This was a considerable financial burden. Another of my life-study lessons: business partnerships (with the exception, perhaps, of those between husband and wife) rarely, if ever, last long term.

Little Claude was only picking up temporary work. Fortunately, Jen had a permanent part-time position and young Sean-Claude was washing dishes in a city restaurant after school.

Over the years, Little Claude kept in contact with his old teenage mates. The one with the dubious distinction of having been thrown off every racecourse in Australia still numbered among them. He now held status in what might be dubbed a 'militant' union. On learning of Little Claude's financial plight, he put in a word for a temporary vacancy at the union office. The grapevine carried optimistic rumours concerning the likelihood of Little Claude's getting the job: they needed someone without a criminal record. (He was the only candidate able to meet such exacting criteria.)

I only ever caught up with my eldest brother at the odd family gathering, so I'm not all that familiar with his inside story. Having made that perfectly clear, I further add that I have never enquired, nor has Little Claude ever proffered an explanation, either to me or to anyone else as to why he was gunned down one morning on his way to work.

He survived with emergency surgery, bearing a scar that made the toes curl to witness. As for emotional scars, he can only hope one day to cultivate some relief from them. (I note an interesting blanching reaction from him whenever a car backfires.)

I can barely imagine how nerve fraying the crass and obtrusive publicity must have been for the family. Especially for Sean-Claude and Claudette who were at school. After a few days, the headlines moved on to another story - leaving the family to make what they could out of the few tattered shreds of normalcy that remained of their lives.

Little Claude eventually found employment in his specific field of expertise. Sean-Claude secured a plumber's apprenticeship as soon as he finished school.

Sean-Claude was competitively involved with the Surf Life-Saving Movement. Both his parents worked tirelessly for his club, spending their weekends at the coast. Claude even took to coaching the Nippers. He quickly became a legend after the rumour spread about the *awesome* scar on his upper body. *It was the only bite the foolish shark could get in before the luckless creature met its untimely end.*

Some years later, the shooting incident came back to haunt Little Claude when unseen bullet fragments worked their way down to his back passage.

Again, he almost died on the operating table from septicaemia.

# Chapter Forty Four

There was a four-lane highway in front of the wrecking yard by the early nineties. This undoubtedly made Ted, and his brother Bill, feel quietly satisfied as they sprawled over dilapidated office chairs, jawing over ways of avoiding pitfalls in the corporate jungle. Ted had made substantial improvements around the place. This included half-a-dozen industrial sheds towards the front boundary and concrete to cover most of the remaining land.

Whilst carrying out the latter task, he became professionally *au fait* with beer prices on the north side, though I doubt he drank much. He came to an arrangement with a number of concrete-mixer drivers, to recycle any excess from local jobs in exchange for a carton. Every day he would have a section boxed up in readiness for superfluous loads. In this way, the entire yard was rapidly swaddled and blanched with concrete. This concrete blanket bore so many indentations that told a story, it was positively hieroglyphic!

The first and only time I ever saw Ted cry was in delivering a eulogy at Bill's funeral. The pair had developed a strong bond over the years, since the time Bill first tracked him down at the orphanage. I recall several stories of Bill and Ted's excellent adventures to Lightning Ridge, in search of that illusive find to set them up for life. I doubt they ever turned up much with their metal-detector, but the companionship was pure gold. Ted always was a man of few words - quietly spoken ones at that. I reckon Bill had been one of scant peers with whom he ever shared a bond.

Ted's sister and her family had lived in Brisbane for many years, by the time Bill passed away. They were at Bill's funeral, as were his brothers who had travelled interstate for the service at Albany Creek crematorium. I hadn't seen them together before and was amazed at the family resemblance. Quite uncanny. Afterwards, everyone returned to their respective routines but, for a long time, Ted seemed to have lost his shadow.

By now he leased the wrecking yard proper, as well as a couple of the big sheds. This provided a reasonable income. It still meant there were sheds left for Bart and Dan who, by then, were virtually self-employed selling car parts and associated activities.

Because Ted's only occupation these days was writing receipts, he regularly devoted himself to giving his son a running commentary on how to manage the business. These inroads of good intention usually ended up in serious testosterone showdowns.

Ted had trouble running at idling speed. When a swanky new estate opened at Bridgeman Downs, his motor changed up a gear. The houses looked like a street-set for *The Truman Show*. Having decided it was time to build a new home, he acquired a parcel of land. Then he set about almost single-handedly constructing a still ritzier version of their home at Aspley. Before Patrice had a chance to unpack from the move, he was laying the foundations to a splendid residence for his son, on a block up the street.

Ted worked seven days a week. Tony and I would drop over on Sundays for the mandatory guided site-tour and chat. On one such occasion at Bart's work in progress, Ted quietly suggested he was happy to work for the cost of materials if Bart threw in a packet of smokes and a pie every day.

Ted was truly one of life's gems.

# Chapter Forty Five

For the first time in 70 years, Christmas dinner of 1995 was held outside The Grand House. Some fine theatrical performances were staged to convince mum to entrust the MC's task to one of her daughters. We no longer saw Jen and Little Claude every Christmas. Since Claudette's marriage, she had moved onto a cane farm in North Queensland. Little Claude and Jen now spent every second Christmas with their daughter, and '95 was an *up there* year.

I drew the short straw to put on the first Christmas away from The Grand House, so I was quietly thankful this year was an *up* one. At least the chaos wouldn't be quite so overwhelming. My idea of having a barbecue, or cold meat and salad went over like a bouffant at a festival of earth mothers. Mum ensured the traditional stayed firmly implanted in Christmas dinner. Everything fell into place without a hitch and I gladly handed the baton on to Patrice to run with in '96.

Everyone was expected for the following year's festivities, the venue being Patrice's mansion at Bridgeman Downs. She spent valuable time away from tripping the light fantastic to establish the gardens. She wanted the place to look perfect by the time Christmas dinner '96 came around.

In the October of '96, Ted had a blackout. He was working with Bart at some minor task at the wrecking yards. He took off to his doctor.

Patrice had that sinking feeling when the doctor asked them both into the surgery. Ted's first reaction was to tell nobody the dreadful news. I really don't know how I would react in the circumstances. Ted loathed the idea of people feeling they had to make a fuss, or to torture their poorly rehearsed theatrical repertoire for expressions of pity.

Within a day or so after the initial shock, he realised Patrice would need moral support. So she was given the nod to tell a chosen few:

Ted had inoperable cancer and wasn't expected to live more than 18 months!

A shock wave reverberated around past and present members of The Grand House. At Ted's specific request, none of his blood relatives were told. This proved awkward when he and Patrice were invited to his sister's fiftieth wedding anniversary; celebrations were scheduled for mid-December '96. They sidestepped the party with a convenient excuse.

That shattering news wasn't the last bomb to be dropped before the shell-shocked troops retreated to the Bridgeman Downs bunker for Christmas dinner '96.

A routine visit to the local quack by mum in early December resulted in an X-ray that picked up a blood clot close to her lung. Fearing a stroke, the doctor hospitalised her for evasive action.

Everything was looking positive after a few days of treatment; that is, until I answered the phone early on Monday the $16^{th}$ of December. A soothing bedside-mannered voice told me my mother was critically ill. The voice belonged to the sister in charge of mum's ward, at Royal Brisbane. Despite my stunned state, I followed her suggestion to notify family and close friends as a matter of urgency. Almost everyone ever associated with The Grand House, including Uncle Fergus's clan rallied to the Royal Brisbane that morning for a bedside vigil.

Ted and Cecelia weren't up to making the pilgrimage, being constrained by their own health. Amazingly, not only did the old girl hang in that day; she slowly edged away from death's door and back through the door of The Grand House. Despite having being squeezed through the wringer, she made it to Christmas dinner.

It was a strange beginning to 'festivities' at Patrice and Ted's. The gathering was virtually comatose on arrival, what with the news of Ted's impending death and mum's close encounter. From a perceived need to snap out of it: everyone spontaneously determined to create a lighthearted atmosphere. Dan and I did our bit when we held the floor.

We told our captive audience about the days immediately preceding mum's release from Royal Brisbane. There had been a unanimous decision (the second in my living memory) to attend to certain urgencies at The Grand House before her return. The first priority was to deal with the ever-expanding population of feral cats that had adopted the place as a safe haven - food always available courtesy of mum.

Next on the list was the thirty-five year old, ailing cockatoo. This sick and sorry old bird would screech like a deranged harpy every evening at dusk, until his cumbersome cage was carried upstairs to the back patio. Then he would make everyone's hair stand on end again, at dawn, until he was returned to his spot under the stairs.

143

Desperate situations require desperate solutions. Dan and I determined to round 'em up and herd them off to the RSPCA before mum arrived home from hospital. Catching a feral cat is no, *here puss, puss.* We rigged a cage, once home to the other cockatoo, which had fallen off his perch (so to speak) a few years earlier. Pitting our wits against the native cunning of felines, we would relocate the trap then lurk for hours behind posts and trees (looking somewhat lamely feral ourselves) waiting for the exact moment to pull the string.

We made at least a half a dozen trips to Fairfield with a couple at a time, eventually incarcerating all but two, skinny, street-wise alley-kittens. Top Cat and Benny continually slipped through a gap in the wire before we could throw the blanket over. For our last drop, we borrowed Ted's ute to transport both the trap, and the old cockatoo in his cage, simultaneously.

Ted's old workhorse ute was, to put it elegantly, a bomb. The front bench-seat had loosened, meaning whenever I hit the brakes the entire cabin space contracted toward the dashboard.

Everyone at Christmas dinner that year chortled to the Ma and Pa Kettle image Dan and I conjured, trundling through the Valley streets and across the Story Bridge in a derelict ute, with a cage full of terrified cats and a screeching, almost featherless cockatoo.

Uncle Fergus, his wife and adult sons joined us that year for Christmas dinner. Great deserts of golden grains had slid through the neck of the hourglass since we last did the Christmassy thing together.

The other wonderful surprise was having Royce's partner along. That was a first! Despite the fifteen or more years they had been an item. Some benefits had come out of mum's close call: she and Roslyn at last broke down the barriers.

And, guess what? Yes, they became the closest of friends.

# Chapter Forty Six

1997 started with a chill wind of impending disaster eerily creaking the veteran timbers of The Grand House (and no less eerily in The Grand House veterans). The paradox was, this should have been anything but a year of despair. In January, Royce was to turn fifty. In March, Dan would reach forty and in April, Ted was due to be celebrating his sixtieth. In May, my son Ben would be eighteen. The score card didn't end there, either. June was my twentieth wedding anniversary. In October, Uncle Fergus would be clocking up seventy years, whilst my mother-in-law would be turning ninety.

In mid-January my mother-in-law, who always was an astoundingly active woman, suffered a stroke. When confronted with the depressing prospect of languishing in a nursing home for good, she deliberated a fortnight, then made the nerve-shattering announcement that she would refuse any further treatment at the Royal Brisbane.

They fed her intravenously, before determining her resolve. She died in mid-March a couple of days after the drips were removed. After saying a last goodbye to his mother, Tony trotted down the hill from Royal Brisbane to the smart offices of K.M. Smith at Bowen Hills, where he arranged his mother's cremation at Albany Creek. Her ashes were returned to Bendigo to be with her late husband.

Yes, I had married one of god's frozen people - a Victorian.

It took about a year before my family and I were on speaking terms again. They eventually came to realise my options were limited. Lacking the classic cover-girl looks of my sister and sister-in-law, it was obvious I could have been pushed to the back of the shelf, then passed over. It could have been worse, I might have married someone from Tasmania or god forbid, even a Kiwi!

Ted's condition deteriorated over the year. His courage was an inspiration to everyone. He quietly yet carefully set his affairs in order, taking advice from his accountant and solicitor. Within a short time, the estate was transferred to Patrice. The wrecking-yard and its sub-lets were signed up on long-term leases, designed to guarantee Patrice an income well into the future.

One shed was left for Bart, as a base for his future business. Even from his wheelchair, Ted continued to give Bart unsolicited advice on how to run his affairs. Bart was never exactly backwards in coming forwards with vividly graphic descriptions of what he could do with his suggestions.

Ted's public outings became less frequent. His last was a quiet family get-together for his sixtieth birthday at his favourite Chinese restaurant at Chermside. He needed to rest most of the afternoon, just to make it through a simple, low-key celebration.

Dan made the selfless decision not to re-open his spare-parts business after Christmas '96, in order to be a round-the-clock carer for mum. Her recovery was slow, her heart now the greatest problem. Dan spent hours shuffling her between the hospital, her private doctor, assorted X-ray clinics and pathologists. None of us were exactly confident she would see another Christmas.

In July, out of the blue, Cecelia joined the waiting list of those determined to check out of life's hotel before Christmas. (By now, I worried these were somewhat desperate ploys to avoid another Christmas at my place.)

For Cecelia, it started when I took her up to casualty at Royal Brisbane after she developed what I thought was simply a nosebleed she couldn't stem. She was admitted to the Renal Ward. The doctor confided that, in his expert opinion, he doubted she had much longer.

I decided to restrict access to that news. I definitely couldn't tell mum, bearing in mind her heart condition (and prevailing circumstances). Dan and I struck some light in the darkness, wagering the odds on whose funeral would be next. This was as we made the daily trek from The Grand House to the Royal Brisbane to visit Cecelia in the Renal Ward and mum, who was in and out of the Coronary Ward.

Patrice was now largely preoccupied with Ted. On his insistence, she found time for regular coffee dates with her friends from dance class. I barely had time to catch up with Ted. When I did make the trip out to Bridgeman Downs, I was staggered by the changes. His had been a burly frame, built through a lifetime of physically demanding work. Now he looked pathetically wasted. It was a slouched skeleton of his former stalwart self that stared back at me, despondently, from his favourite old lounge chair.

In August, the social worker at Royal Brisbane pulled me aside to discuss Cecelia's situation. To put it bluntly, there was nothing more they could do and they needed her bed. Her options were The Grand House or a nursing home. The fiasco at The Grand House meant it was right out. I gently broke the news to Cecelia, reassuring her we would find a pleasant place and she would be visited every day.

Patrice and I scouted around a few dozen neighbourhoods. We put Cecelia's name down anywhere that looked acceptable. Vacancies are plentiful if you can afford the substantial up-front fee and all but non-existent if all you can give is your pension.

A social worker came up with a bed in a place at New Farm.

Cecelia was now seventy-five. For the last thirty-five of those years her sister had been her sole carer. Although Cecelia could rise to the occasion when the situation demanded, her preferred rôle was that of a cantankerous dependant. Now Ella was the one needing care. Cecelia was petrified of facing the world without her sister's support.

Mum was determined to see the nursing home before we accepted; to be assured her sister was moving into pleasant surrounds. She was too emotionally distraught when it came to it, to be part of the transfer from hospital to nursing home. I went alone to help Cecelia settle in. I felt so drained and wretched leaving her weeping that day, with a promise to return the next.

Without fail either Dan or I separately, or together for moral support, spent a part of each subsequent day with Cecelia.

Even Patrice grabbed a moment away from Ted to do likewise. Ted was now in palliative care at Prince Charles Hospital. On the day of her admission to the home, I noted Cecelia's mind was ticking over well, despite her frail body's exhaustion. She answered a variety of questions, without prompting, about her background and medical condition.

Each day I visited, she was less alert. Her condition rapidly deteriorated. I'm not sure whether the change was medication-related or her inability to cope with her situation. Staff at the home told us she wavered between crying and cursing most of the time. Each visit was totally different. One day she would be away with the pixies, the next she spoke with remarkable clarity.

I took mum for a visit one day, which proved not the wisest move. Cecelia was incommunicado, frequently confusing reality with dreams. Mum broke down on witnessing the enormous deterioration of her sister's mental state, in the short time since they last talked.

I was undergoing a surreal, mind-warping phase with these two close family members simultaneously staring their own mortality in the face, a few kilometres from each other. Anyone close to them was flat out trying to stay sane and positive. Ted was definitely accepting his fate with more dignity than Cecelia, which comment is not intended to be disparaging. I have no idea how I'll handle this trauma.

Despite Ted's having made it abundantly clear he wanted nobody, apart from Patrice and Bart, to see him in those despairing final stages, something compelled me to call in one Sunday afternoon. As soon as I saw the pathetic little figure of my sister, sitting alone by her husband's bed, I felt my decision to go against Ted's wishes had been vindicated. I doubt, anyway, he was aware of my presence.

Patrice and I sat together by Ted's bed for a few hours. I can't even remember what we spoke about. I returned again on the Monday, when Bart was present. The three of us laughed nervously about different things.

Walking out of the ward with Patrice late that afternoon, I assured her I would be back tomorrow. She must have had a gut feeling there would be no tomorrow for Ted. She told me later she had a quick coffee, then resumed her bedside vigil. He clung to life long enough for Bart to return and be with him at the end, which was at two the next morning.

K.M. Smith was called upon again to make the arrangements for Ted at Albany Creek Crematorium. The service was held on Friday the 19th of September. It was a highly charged, emotional experience to watch Little Claude deliver a moving eulogy for his brother-in-law and lifelong friend.

Mum was readmitted to Coronary Care the following day.

The most bizarre part of the entire episode was when Patrice tried to contact Ted's surviving brothers, who lived interstate, about his death. There had been no communication between any of them since Bill's funeral a few years earlier.

Patrice was dumbfounded to learn they too had died *within a few days of Ted.*

The day after Ted's service, Dan and I called on Cecelia, having spent a few minutes with mum in the Coronary Ward. Cecelia was remarkably lucid on that occasion, even enquiring as to how Patrice was holding up after Ted's death. We were staggered! We had been far from certain she would remember anything. Patrice paid Cecelia a visit the next day, Sunday. Then, on Monday morning, I received a call: Cecelia passed away during the night.

It felt like proof of nature's boundless compassion having mum in Coronary Care, when Patrice and I had to deliver this knockabout tiding. We first spoke to the sister-in-charge, who gave us the green light. With everything else going on around her, no-one had told mum the full story about her sister's state of health, so the news of Cecelia's death after less than a fortnight in the nursing home caught her completely off guard.

By midday, Patrice and I were back down at K.M. Smith. Cecelia was buried one week to the day after Ted, by which time mum had been released from hospital.

Christmas '97 came round with no further casualties at The Grand House. A common topic with all and sundry was what a shocker of a year it had been. Dinner was at Royce and Roslyn's house, of all places.

Roslyn had by now formed an amazingly close bond with mum, hardly surprising considering their similarities. During their fifteen-year *cold war* they rarely made contact. Now, suddenly, mum was over their place every Friday night, watching the trots on their large-screen TV and giving the phone-betting account a terrific workout.

Improvements in mum's health allowed Dan to resume fulltime employment. He was offered a position in a family company owned by one of Ted's closest friends, from his old speedway days.

In hindsight, that devastating year was probably the catalyst for this book. We come into the world, carry out our prescribed tasks and then die. The suffering this involves drives most to religion, materialism, intoxication, addiction, automatism, violence, treachery, madness, hatred or despair.

Few tread the tightrope of moderation, compassion and reason.

I suppose we're lucky to feel the pathos of it all at any age.

You only have to pick up a newspaper or turn on the television to see the way death is now flooding out lives like a tsunami. '97 seemed a particularly *in your face* splash for noteworthy departures. Princess Di immediately springs to mind. Mother Teresa was another. It's as if they weren't foolish enough to venture into the unchartered waters of this coming millennium. We fools rushed in - where angels feared to tread.

It's easy to be philosophical about death when the deceased is a name or face in the news. It's tougher when death strikes close to home. As the song-writer Hal David wrote, way back in the sixties,

*What's it all about, Alfie?*

The lyrical nuance of that question has remained with me, with no taint of an answer to compromise the melody of its scepticism.

# Chapter Forty Seven

Quite a few familiar faces pulled out of the race to the new millennium during the last, far lap of the nineties. The Old Man's childhood-friend Declan Murphy being a prime example.

Death for him must have been a blissful release. I can't remember ever hearing him laugh. He would struggle to raise half a crippled smile as he tagged along behind his domineering little wife, his ears bleeding from her ceaseless nagging. At the time of his demise, he had long since retired from the labourer's job he diligently toiled at, for as far back as my memory stretches. To the end, he undertook regular voluntary cleaning and maintenance work around the parish church (any excuse to get out of the house). The priest put on a good sendoff party for him.

Mickey O'Rourke's eldest girl, Grace was also a late scratching. She had never married; instead she devoted her life to keeping house for her bachelor brothers who were totally devastated at her late withdrawal from the race. Oddly enough, I had an opportunity to get to know her towards the end of her life, despite the age gap.

She worked for longer than she cared to remember in the bottle shop of The Victory Hotel in the city, just round the corner from where my Tony worked. He was a regular customer (alas) and one day I happened to go in with him. It took a few sideways glances before the penny dropped. Once we realised the long connection between our two families, we suddenly found ourselves cantering over vast tracts of conversational ground. She was a real trooper. I fully appreciate why she's so sorely missed by her brothers.

I was saddened when the news filtered through - quite awhile after the fact - Karl had also passed away. Karl left the job at the factory not long after I married and he and Royce subsequently lost contact. Royce only heard news of his death after someone pinned it to the factory noticeboard. Karl would only have been in his early forties when he died, which isn't a particularly long innings these days. I can only presume it was his kidney condition.

Mr. and Mrs. Wood both called it a day before the end of the millennium. They had packed their oilskins and tarpaulins and were braving another return to Australia, having purchased the loftiest raised-house in Chermside. At least they had finally reached a decision as to where they wanted to spend the rest of their lives, even if it was only to drown in the millennial tsunami.

I'm almost ashamed to admit, considering how kind the couple was to my family and me, I don't even know when Mr. & Mrs. C. withdrew from the race. I recall seeing Mrs. C. some years ago. I was visiting mum at The Grand House when she dropped in on her way home from the Valley, where she often went for a quiet drink. (Apparently she had worked up quite a routine in this respect during her latter years. That gave the tongues of the god-bothering bigots in the street something to waggle about.)

I haven't even tried to get to the bottom of the rumour about Errol-John finding himself on the wrong side of the law. I really don't give a damn, preferring the memory I have of the loveable larrikin who called me Bubba.

Two elderly spinster nieces of the local councillor-cum-benevolent shopkeeper remained in the race almost to the end. They were the same ducks who gave Dan and Bart such grief for marking the footpath with their billy-cart. The younger one, whom I realised wasn't a bad old dear once I got to know her, passed away just before the farthest lap, in late '99. She was totally worn out from being a carer to her elder, invalid sister about whom I knew little, except that she continues to reside alone up the street to this day.

The little old White Russian lady two doors up (affectionately know as Mrs. Kwit because I could never pronounce her name) was only a month off crossing the line when she finally succumbed to a long illness, in November '99. She was a real darling who definitely didn't draw an easy barrier position in life's race. She fought like a Tartar to the end. The strength of character she would have built from enduring a Nazi concentration camp was learned, too, as her parents had escaped the Bolsheviks in Russia when she was a tiny tot.

Her husband hanged himself back in the late seventies.

I know this because Royce was still living at home when Mrs. Kwit rushed in to plead for assistance with cutting the body from where it was suspended, turning white and anti-clockwise. Mr. and Mrs. Kwit remind me of that wonderful SBS series called *Tales from a Suitcase*. It takes so much bloody-minded courage to start a new life in a 'remote' country where nothing resembles the blissful scenes, impressed like nostalgia on the mind's eye of the child.

They flee war, poverty, violence or family feuds given the slenderest chance their children might realise a more productive and harmonious life. I believe Mr. & Mrs. Kwit's grandchildren are highly specialised medical and legal professionals.

As the 1990s drew to a close, my mind often spanned over the last century of evolution. When Grandfather Fred from Kent, young Jewish Rebecca from Cromer, the Fitzgeralds from County Cork and the O'Hoynes (Nanny's parents) from Godknowswhere on the Emerald Isle traversed the oceans of half the world.

In reflection, I feel an immense gratitude for their long, arduous and often perilous voyage to this Great Southern Land. The pioneering spirit, their braving the privation of being removed from emotional support (often of a kind you're not aware exists, until it has gone) is breathtaking to imagine. Regardless of whether it was the gold in the ground or the gold of pristine sandy beaches under a warm sun which lured them: the true gold was discovered when their hearts fell in love with the dream of being here.

I feel pleased about the successive waves of migration that followed my grandparents. I salivate at the mere thought of eating at a particular Greek Taverna in Boundary Street. West End is crammed with other equally fine cafés, restaurants, bistros and bakeries operated by people from Greece to Vietnam. Our climate begs to be culturally developed along Mediterranean-cum-tropical lines. Let the flow of migration continue to enrich our lives. The sole prerequisite for acceptance to the fold being first and foremost, a pacifist conviction.

# Finale

Those of us directly linked to The Grand House, who managed to survive the familial holocaust of '97, continued through to make it to the new millennium in tact. That almost excluded Uncle Fergus: one of his lungs was ripped out in October of '99, following a cancer scare. The only Y2K disaster happened to Royce. Adhering to a community announcement suggesting the bath be filled in case of water-supply problems after midnight; he forgot he left the tap on until Roslyn noticed flooding down the hallway.

Almost forty years after Mr. C. put in a good word for him, Royce continues to toil away at the only job he has ever known. Every morning and evening you can find him feeding and brushing his pampered Kojak that, notwithstanding sixteen years on the hoof, has never borne the brunt of a saddle on his back.

Little Claude phoned mum early on New Millennium's Eve. When she heard the dulcet tones of, 'Hello, Mummy!' she knew her eldest boy was already well into the celebrations. (Little Claude only does *inner-child* when he's sloshed.) Little Claude inherited quite a few of Paddy's characteristics, especially the Irish tendency to look for a fight after a few too many.

Young Sean-Claude came down from his employment in New Guinea to enter the new millennium with his parents. They now live on the coast, close to the surf club where Sean-Claude is a life member. In a strange way history repeats itself, as Sean-Claude contends with the plethora of excuses levelled at him - Whitey Boss Man - by his gang of native workers. They are generally indifferent to the Protestant work-ethic. (One poor fellow had been to his own mother's funeral three times since Sean-Claude took him on.)

He lives in Port Moresby in a home overlooking the bay. His panoramic vista takes in what's left of the submerged wreck of a hospital ship, bombed by the Japanese during the war. Ella is reasonably confidant her brother Jack was onboard at the time.

He also took the opportunity to visit Rabaul. The Chinatown where that last photo of his Great Uncle Jack was taken no longer exists. However, there's a plaque bearing his name on a war memorial in the area.

Claudette has been living in North Queensland for so long now, I doubt she could cope with the chilling pace of life in the Great Southeast. The eldest of her four daughters started high school in 2000.

Despite her sixty years, Patrice doesn't stop between helping Bart at his shed and rehearsing for the next dance concert. Mum loves to watch her firstborn daughter dance these days, just as she loved to watch her baby daughter forty years earlier. I never felt any overpowering urge to dig out the dancing shoes again.

These days I put in a token amount of time in voluntary work for the homeless and addicted. I suppose it's an attempt to clear my conscience about the way I handled the situation with my father and his brother all those years ago. Being an atheist puts the responsibility of conscience directly in your own hands. There's no hypocrisy of appealing for forgiveness, and I'm absolutely not motivated by some vain delusion of gaining myself a peachy-creamy possie in heaven. I'm proud to be a Born-Again Heathen. Hallelujah! I've seen the light. It's a positively liberating experience.

Mickey O'Rourke's youngest son, Shamus dropped in to The Grand House over Christmas to pay his respects to mum. This is something he has done every year since they were children, although I think he's past doing the traditional cartwheel down the hall, nowadays. He's a relic of a bygone era when you went to the honesty-box at the end of the street for the morning paper. A shy, quiet, gentle man, he wouldn't tell you so himself, but he was presented with a Community Service Award for his tireless work at the local Catholic primary school and church. He continues to live just up the road with his two bachelor brothers. The three of them rely on meals-on-wheels, since their sister Grace died. (One orders booze-on-wheels, courtesy of the local hotel's free delivery service!)

I gave Shamus O'Rourke a lift out to the Albany Creek Crematorium a couple of times, when we were dispatching neighbours who fell short of the finish line in the race to two thousand. I was staggered at the information this bloke has stored in his lovely, leprechaun-sized head. Information pertaining to films and movie stars dating back to the earliest classics shown at the Crystal Palace. He would definitely give David Stratton a run for his money. He also told mum he has been to Disneyland and Ireland. In his dreams, these two places frequently become confused. He didn't enjoy Ireland after someone stole his clothes (it had to have been a leprechaun - they

154

wouldn't fit anyone else). On the other hand, he was so enthralled with Disneyland that he made a return trip.

I have a mental picture of this miniature character, spinning in the teacup ride with a big Irish grin. He might easily have been mistaken for one of the rôle-playing characters employed to roam the place for 'atmosphere'. Unlike his brother, who orders booze by the wagonload, Shamus takes a quiet drink every Saturday morning at the Crown Hotel, with the younger son from Mrs. C.'s first marriage. The latter continues to reside four doors up from The Grand House, where we used to take refuge from the floods and watch *Leave It to Beaver* on Sunday nights.

In another blast from the past, mum had a phone call out of the blue from Paul Maroney. He needed to tell Little Claude something after forty years. I don't know whether he managed to track him down, or if the urgency to communicate simply passed. Paul's younger brother, Neville, who intimidated me so much when I was a child, dropped in to The Grand House around the same time. It seems he was taking a final twirl around the neighbourhood where he grew up before moving permanently to San Francisco, where his interior decorating business really took off.

Mum spends most of her days alone at The Grand House now, surrounded by photos and memories. Memories of when the walls reverberated with the sound of Irish ditties, children's laughter and fighting. Piano sing-a-longs and rollicking rock 'n' roll records vied for attention with Cecelia's incessant complaint about her aches and pains. All she wished for back then was a bit of peace and quiet.

Don't wish too hard for what you want. You just might find you don't really want it after all.

Mum will indeed see her youngest grandson Ben turn twenty-one, in May 2000. That'll be a wonderful outcome, in the light of her wistful comment when he was a baby. She has nothing like the stamina of a few years ago, walking with a stick, angina tablets never far from reach. The doctors have told her nothing short of major heart surgery will alleviate the condition (but the chances of her surviving that sort of trauma are remote). We're all blatantly aware she's now living on borrowed time and it probably wont be long until she's pushing up waratahs. When the inevitable happens, I imagine Patrice will sell The Grand House and it will be demolished for redevelopment.

Its only value these days is the land. No longer flood-prone, after extensive and obviously successful flood-mitigation work was performed following the '74 inundation. When that happens, all that will remain of The Grand House are these few chapters and those photos, which I intend to personally and carefully remove from the dining room wall for posterity.

I wonder what the backhoe operator will think when he comes across the old T-Model buried under the mango tree.